Auction In Zunguzonga

Sustainable Development Deferred

by

I. Chukuma Onwueme

authorHOUSE™

1663 LIBERTY DRIVE, SUITE 200
BLOOMINGTON, INDIANA 47403
(800) 839-8640
WWW.AUTHORHOUSE.COM

© 2005 I. Chukuma Onwueme. All Rights Reserved.

First published by AuthorHouse 03/08/05

ISBN: 1-4208-2768-5 (sc)

Printed in the United States of America
Bloomington, Indiana

This book is printed on acid-free paper.

Dedication

To Naidene and Thomas Evans
To a Future of Peace through Equity in our shared Humanity
To Hope for all those who are down

Acknowledgement

I would like to acknowledge the following persons who reviewed the manuscript at one stage or another: George Baumgardner, Michael Cornelius, Udoka Onwueme, Jan Warner, and Ebele Onwueme (the original Bedemu). I am grateful for their comments and suggestions. I also acknowledge the filial moral support of Kenolisa (Bangumba), Kiki, Baabundo, and Malijane.

Damaged Goods

Who, in all sincerity,
In all honesty and veracity,
Can claim that their baggage is unblemished?
No!
On close examination,
We're all, without exception,
Damaged goods.

I. C. Onwueme (1997)

x

Chapter 1 – A curious trio

The three men walked briskly. They had parked their car nearly half a kilometre from their intended destination. Now, they were picking their way through the pockmarked pathway that passed for a street. Bicycles, pedestrians, street vendors and the occasional car jostled for right of way. The monsoon rain of the previous night had filled each pothole on the street, creating a patchwork of reddish puddles that splashed unmercifully at pedestrians as each vehicle navigated the maze. Both sides of the street were lined with two or three-storey residential buildings in which the ground floor invariably doubled as commercial premises for traders, tailors, barbers, cobblers and other small-time professionals. As the group of three went by, they were approached several times by various artisans soliciting their business. But the men kept a studied silence, only barely signalling to the traders and artisans that they were not interested in what they had to offer.

The oldest and shortest of the men was clad in a dark business suit. The fabric of the suit, though relatively new, was stretched taut in all directions from the ample flesh that it tried to rein in. The man was already panting, and sweating profusely from the brisk pace of the walk. Beads of sweat were forming on his balding pate, coalescing, and gushing down his face in rivulets. A handkerchief was on duty to soak up the rivulets, just as more formed to replace them. Every few steps, the man would hunch his shoulders in a desperate attempt to catch a deep breath. He went by the rather unusual name of Mr. Skoop. Whether or not it was an alias, nobody around could say for sure, but that was what everybody called him.

The second man, younger and taller, was also clad in a western-style suit. His body was adorned in considerable ornamentation: a dangling gold necklace, a matching bracelet on the left wrist, and a ring on the index finger of each hand. A shiny golden tie-clasp held a broad, flowery tie in place. His gait had a rhythmic swagger, to match his narcissistic mien. Curiously, he carried a shiny, medium-sized hand bell, smothered in a blue napkin to prevent it from clanging as its carrier went along.

The third man wore a simple grey native jumper, much the worse for wear, but still enough to embellish his otherwise scrawny frame. For footwear, he had a pair of brown sandals, the left one of which was unbuckled, flapping rhythmically against the sole of his foot as he walked. He was clean-shaven: jaw, chin, lip, head and all. This man trailed a couple of steps behind his two companions, and somehow seemed the least enthusiastic about whatever mission the triumvirate was up to.

The trio made a left turn at the petrol station, proceeded for another fifty metres or so, and then pulled to an abrupt halt. The two men in suits glanced at each other as if to ask: "What do I do now?" They exchanged reciprocal nods of reassurance. The man with the bell then pulled out a sheet of paper from his pocket, consulted it for a second, and then with all the flourish and force he could muster, he clanged his bell, loud and clear, but only once. He turned to the other two, exchanged cursory smiles with them, then swung around and began walking back towards their car. The others followed. The pace on this return journey was no less brisk. The short fat man, now at the limits of his physical endurance, was no longer able to keep up with the other two, and was quite content to bring up the rear.

When he heard the bell ring on the street below, Keli Alili peered out of his upstairs window, and caught a glimpse of the trio just before they turned around to proceed on their return journey. He watched them for a few seconds, and then called out to his wife, Dada, who was then in the kitchen.

"Achoo!" he exclaimed, uttering a meaningless expression that, since childhood, had been his own peculiar way of reacting to exciting or surprising situations. "DD! Come! Come quickly. Come and see what's happening on our street. It's yet another one of those fringe religious groups in the town. This time, it seems that they're operating on our street."

Dada came running out to join Keli on the balcony.

3

"Those fake prophets are all over the place, especially here in Magotown," Keli continued.

"Yes," replied Dada. "It seems that they can't find enough souls to convert."

"They are not serious. Many of them are simply unemployed city folk looking for a way to make quick money."

"Everybody is out to make quick money these days," said Dada.

"And they will do it by whatever means, fair or foul," Keli added.

"It's too bad. The youth of today just want to make money. And they're very impatient about it. They want the money, and they want it now. Nothing like ethics or morality in their money-making drive."

Together, the husband and wife watched the trio until they again rounded the corner near the petrol station and disappeared from view.

"You know something?" Dada said, suddenly turning to Keli. "I think I've seen this group before."

"Where? In your dreams?"

"No. I think I saw them yesterday."

"You must be joking."

"No joking. I saw them."

"Where?"

"When I went to buy vegetables at the market. They were operating there. They had a prostitute kneeling on the ground, with a large crowd surrounding them. It seems that they were trying to cast the devil from the prostitute."

"Ohhh! Not the old exorcism trick?"

"Something like it. They doused the prostitute with holy water, and the preacher subjected her to a barrage of incantations. At the height of the ritual, the prostitute fainted. At least she pretended to faint."

"Then what?"

"At this point, the incantations reached a crescendo, and more holy water was administered. Then the prostitute suddenly stood up and declared herself to have been born again. The crowd roared with approbation."

"Were you convinced?"

"Me? Not at all. I wasn't convinced. I suspected that both the prostitute and the exorcist could have belonged to the same group of con artists. It is a strange world, isn't it?"

"Indeed. A world full of desperate people eager to dupe you."

"Only a fool can fall for their tricks. Nobody falls for that kind of trickery these days."

"Apparently, enough people fall for it to keep them in business. Otherwise, we wouldn't be seeing so many of the dupes."

Keli laughed. Dada laughed. And the event they had just watched on the street was allowed to pass from their consciousness. Dada returned to the kitchen, while Keli splayed himself out comfortably on the sofa in the upstairs balcony of the house.

Keli was on annual vacation leave from his job as Deputy Director at the Ministry of Foreign Affairs, and was enjoying every minute of it. As the civil servant with the second highest rank in the Ministry, he had been denied the opportunity to take leave for the past couple of years; what with the interminable string of foreign trips he had had to undertake as an indispensable member of the foreign minister's team. Repeated requests for his annual leave were invariably pushed aside by one or other of the inevitable emergencies that the foreign ministry had to juggle all the time. It verged on the unpatriotic for him to insist on taking leave during such times, and Keli usually did not press his requests for leave too strenuously. Keli was not indispensable, but he was very much close to it.

This year, though, things were slightly different. He was allowed the bare minimum of six weeks leave, and was bent on enjoying every minute of it. This was the second week of his leave, and things seemed to be going pretty well. On this particular day, the oppressive tropical heat was just beginning to set in, and he was lolling about, reading and re-reading the day's newspapers. The news consisted of the same unchanging gloomy staple that he and his fellow citizens of Zunguzonga had become used to: the dire straits into which the economy of this third world country had fallen, the precipitous rise in unemployment, the plunging value of the zungu (ZZ, the national currency), the inevitable increase in criminality, the insidious impact of corruption on society; nothing much to make you smile or to lift your spirits. The only silver lining to the cloudy picture was the enduring sweetness and extensive reportage relating to the recent string of victories by the national soccer team.

Oh, yes, the national team! This team seemed incapable of putting a foot wrong with their all-conquering brand of football. In a country where suffering and deprivation were egregiously palpable, the football team was indeed proving to be a veritable opium of the people. It was a panacea that simultaneously delivered analgesic and hallucinogenic remedy to relieve the misery of a maligned populace.

By noon of the day after the bell-ringing incident, Keli and Dada were no longer laughing. They were gearing up for a late breakfast. The rice on the stove was ready and steaming; but the curry sauce to go with it still had a couple of minutes to simmer. While Dada cooked, Keli was seeing to the placement of the cutlery, napkins and drinking glasses on the small dining table. Suddenly, a loud knock at the door caused them to put all arrangements on hold. Keli, still in his pyjamas, scurried into the bedroom to put on more decent clothes. Dada snuffed out the heat from the cooking stove, shoved utensils back into their cupboard, and for good measure, suffused the room with air freshener spray intended to mask the odour of the late-morning curry she had been preparing. When the frenzy subsided, the couple felt that they were ready for whomever had chosen to visit at that awkward time. Keli opened the door, gingerly. It was Mr. Skoop. He seemed faintly familiar, but Keli could not quite place him. And the visitor was not alone. Standing behind him was a tall, impeccably dressed young man with bushy hair, a thin moustache, and heavy, horn-rimmed glasses. He was totally unfamiliar to Keli. He stood behind Mr. Skoop, and was clumsily clutching a brown briefcase so heavily engorged with documents that the zipper was forced to remain open. This dapper fellow was Mr. Skoop's lawyer.

Not knowing who these people were, Keli was reluctant to let them into the house. He was content to stand in the doorway, while the visitors stood outside, at least until their mission became clearer. Perfunctory greetings were exchanged, and the visiting pair introduced themselves, half-heartedly. They seemed to be in a hurry, and wasted no time in announcing why they were there. The lawyer spoke for the pair.

"We are here to give you this notice."

"What notice?" asked Keli

"Notice for you to vacate this house within three weeks."

"Achoo! Are you crazy?" retorted Keli. "Vacate which house?"

"This house. This house belongs to my client here."

"You must be mistaken."

"No, we're not. Is this not No. 44 Bangumba Street?"

"Yes?"

"This house now belongs to my client. I have all the papers here to prove it."

Keli could not believe his ears. His first instinct was to retreat back into the house and slam the door in their face, but he restrained himself. In a half-hearted attempt to confirm the legitimacy of the visiting pair, he asked the lawyer to show him the documentation that had conferred ownership of the house on Mr. Skoop. The lawyer was only too glad to oblige. He reached into the crowded depths of his briefcase and came up with the required document. Keli took it, glanced at it momentarily, and in fit of rejection and contempt, flung it back in the lawyer's face.

"You must be dreaming," he shouted. "Get away from my house. Both of you can go to hell."

"We, go to hell?" retorted the lawyer. "I have to warn you that…."

Keli did not allow him to complete the sentence. He terminated the visit abruptly, retreated back into the house, and banged the door behind him with a fury that shook this poor contentious house to its foundations. The children were not at home, so Keli felt free to let his anger explode in innumerable and unmentionable expletives, some of which made even Dada cringe in embarrassment.

"Who on earth do these people think they are!" he roared, trembling with rage. "Damn them, I say! Damn them!!"

He was now pacing furiously up and down the living room. Dada followed him around, but at a safe distance to escape his flailing arms.

"Calm down, KK. Calm down," she entreated repeatedly. "Who were those people? What did they say?"

"You call those 'people'. They are animals. Greedy animals!"

"What did they want?"

Keli paused, as he gathered up his emotions for an answer.

"They want our house," he shouted.

"Our house?"

"Yes! This house. We spend all our life's savings to buy a house, and some greedy idiots try to dispossess us of it. To hell with them!"

9

Dada ultimately succeeded in nursing Keli back from the height of his rage. He slumped into his favourite lounge chair, staring blankly into space like a comatose patient. He wondered whether it was he himself, rather than the visitors, that was dreaming.

Chapter 2 – The way to 44 Bangumba Street

Keli had owned the house at No. 44 Bangumba Street for the past nine years. For nearly a decade before that, he was unable to afford a house of his own, or to find a bank that would consider him a fair risk to lend him money to buy one. Apart from occasional stints in government staff quarters, Keli had spent all of his working life renting accommodation. He found this situation particularly painful, partly because of the exorbitant rents that landlords charged, and partly because several of his mates and friends had been able to buy houses of their own. Indeed, the ultimate indignity came during a period when Keli was renting from a fellow civil servant who was several levels his junior in age, rank, salary, and qualification. It was this indignity, coupled with frequent nocturnal entreaties by Dada, that eventually drove Keli into one more desperate effort to secure a loan to buy his own house.

As in previous futile efforts, the first task was to identify a house that was on the market for sale. The newspapers were full of houses being advertised for sale, but only few of these offers were genuine and above board. Most of the houses so advertised usually had a kink or two associated with them, and only a true real estate professional could navigate the treacherous pitfalls that lay on the way. Many of Keli's colleagues at the Ministry were already house owners, and were only too willing to provide advice and guidance to Keli as to how to proceed. For every need in Magotown, there always seemed to be somebody willing and able to supply the need. In this case, the man to see was Juwe Galena.

Juwe was an affable, middle-aged man, much given to drinking and partying. His eyes were frequently blood-shot. This, combined with very bushy eyebrows and a pudgy frame, made him look almost like a circus clown; except when he smiled. His charming smile usually progressed to a boisterous laughter that often singled him out as the life of the party. He had a way with women; indeed he found them irresistible. His amorous ways had caused him to marry while still a teenager. This first marriage ended in divorce. A subsequent marriage also ended in divorce, with his extra-marital liaisons featuring prominently in each of the two divorces.

Juwe lived comfortably, and was well known in Magotown, this city of so many prominent government and business personalities. His main identity was as a professional mechanic who operated the "Junk to

Juwel Vehicle Servicing Workshop" on the outskirts of town. But his real claim to affluence and influence came from an unregistered business that he operated on the side. It was a one-stop shopping real-estate business, if ever there was one. Juwe could help you to find a house, link you up to the loans manager at the bank, and give you a reasonably high level of assurance that your loan application would succeed. His track record among Keli's colleagues, and the general public, attested to his effectiveness. Never mind that clients had to pay exorbitantly for his services; and that much of this payment went as unofficial gratification to the loans manager at the bank. This particular loans manager happened to be Juwe's cousin. Gordon Galena was virtually unapproachable except through Juwe. That, indeed, was the source of Juwe's power and influence in the community, not to mention being the source of wealth so obviously flaunted by Juwe and Gordon.

Keli resolved to seek out Juwe. On the last Saturday in May, he convinced himself that his car needed an oil change, and that Juwe's workshop was just the place to get the work done. He drove down to Juwe's workshop. The place consisted of a reception room, an adjoining spare parts store that also doubled as an office for Juwe, and several contiguous sheds constructed entirely of corrugated iron sheets. Some half-dozen cars lay in various stages of dismemberment in the sheds, while one straddled the mechanic's pit located behind the office.

Keli parked in front of the workshop and proceeded to the reception area. There he was met by one of the senior mechanics.

"You come for servicing, Sir?" the mechanic asked.

"Not full servicing. Just an oil change."

"Oil change," the mechanic repeated, as he scribbled down the instructions. "Anyway, we'll do the normal safety check just to make sure everything is alright."

"Thank you."

"Can I have the keys, Sir?"

"Here. By the way, where is your boss?"

"He's busy inside the office, but he will be out shortly."

"Thanks."

Having commissioned the job on his car, Keli waited for the opportune time to address the real purpose of his visit. Juwe emerged from the office after about ten minutes, and Keli immediately took his chance.

"It seems you've got a lot of business this morning," Keli ventured.

"Yes. Saturdays are always like that. It's always been that way as long as I can remember."

"You've been living in Magotown for long?" Keli asked

"Very long. In fact I practically grew up in this town."

"What of this workshop; have you been operating it for long?"

"About six years."

"It must be very lucrative."

"Not really, but we manage. What's one to do?"

"But things are improving, aren't they?"

"Yes and no. With fewer and fewer people able to afford cars these days, our customer base is shrinking. Very few customers. But the few customers we have cannot afford to buy new cars. So, they keep managing and patching up their old cars, which inevitably break down so very often. That means our workshop is always busy doing repairs. We welcome the business."

"I see."

"On balance, times are very hard. I have even contemplated closing down the workshop and returning to my native village to farm."

Pleasantries over, Keli went straight to the point of his visit.

"A friend of mine told me that you can help people who are looking to buy a house."

"Oh? Who was that?"

"Never mind who it was; but I think it's true. I myself am looking for a house in Magotown for me and my family."

Juwe looked up and fixed a piercing gaze into Keli's eyes. This was a gaze of assessment; double assessment. He was trying to assess whether Keli might be some kind of under-cover law officer on a mission to punch a hole in Juwe's lucrative but shady business. Secondly, the gaze was to assess whether Keli had sufficient financial heft to make him worthy of Juwe's investment of time and energy needed for a real estate transaction. Experience had taught him not to waste his time on financial featherweights who often would not or could not follow through on their transactions.

15

The brief icy gaze froze the dialog while it lasted. When this incisive gaze had mellowed sufficiently, Keli felt emboldened to continue.

"Do you know of any houses up for sale?" asked Keli, unsure of the results of Juwe's assessment. However, Juwe's response was reassuring, and indicated that there was indeed a way forward.

"What kind of house are you interested in?"

"A modest family house will do for me. I cannot really afford those big mansions."

"You want something you can pay for right away?"

"Not exactly. I'll be needing a loan as well. Can you help with that too?" Keli asked, as if he did not know that Juwe's real estate transactions were usually a package deal.

"Do you think you can help with the loan?" Keli was repeating himself.

"We will see how things go," replied Juwe.

There was a pause of a minute or so, while each person pondered the next step. Juwe was the first to break the silence.

"I know of a couple of houses around town that may meet your needs."

"Right here in Magotown?"

"Right here."

"Good. Maybe we can go and take a look at them."

"Sure. I'm busy at the workshop today, so I cannot show you round right away. But tomorrow, Sunday, the workshop is closed, and we can drive around and have a look."

16

"Achoo! Thank you."

This was precisely the kind of appointment that Keli had hoped for. They agreed to meet at 2 p.m. on Sunday, to look at several houses that were in Juwe's portfolio.

When Keli returned home that afternoon, he could barely wait to brief Dada about the actions he had initiated. In previous efforts at getting a house and a loan, Keli had practically tried to go it alone, and the results had been disastrous. Now, his approach was different. He had enlisted the services of someone with a proven track record of producing results. He and Dada were hopeful that with this new approach, success was only a matter of time; a very short time.

"I can see the light at the end of the tunnel," Keli enthused.

"I pray that this nightmare should end soon," Dada responded.

"Hopefully, the final journey starts tomorrow. I can't wait."

"At least there's hope."

"DD, I'm sure you don't mind coming along on the house-hunting drive tomorrow."

"How could I mind? I'm just as excited as you are."

"Good."

"I'll try to prepare lunch early, so we'll be ready when he comes at two."

Chapter 3 – Do you see what you like?

Shortly after 1 p.m. on Sunday, Juwe arrived at Keli's apartment. He was early. He explained that he had another client to attend to at 4 p.m., and wanted to allow ample time for his drive-around with Keli. Dada and Keli hastily prepared themselves for the outing, and joined Juwe in his car.

Of the two houses Juwe showed them that day, the first was a sprawling six-room mansion, with an extensive yard to match. Keli and Dada drooled at the possibility of owning such a house.

"It's nice, isn't it?" Juwe said, as he ushered them through the ornate corridors.

"Very nice," chorused Keli and Dada.

"Yes, this is precisely the kind of house that befits your personality and your position in government. You will be proud, and your entire family will be proud."

"Sure," said Keli. "Who doesn't like a good thing? But I suspect this place must cost a fortune. What is the asking price?"

"This one goes for Z̶Z̶ 650,000. It is really a give-away price."

"Give-away price? Achoo! Give-away or not, that's a pretty hefty price." He glanced at Dada, and added, "I don't think we can afford this one." Dada nodded in agreement.

"Don't be scared of the price," insisted Juwe. "Several of your colleagues own houses like this one. I can even help you to arrange a loan to cover it."

The lure did not work. Sensing that this might be the thin edge of the wedge, Keli and Dada declined to consider this house further. It was clearly beyond their means.

The second house they inspected was a modest three-bedroom affair. Downstairs, the house had one bedroom, in addition to the living room and kitchen; upstairs, there were two bedrooms and an adjoining balcony. The house, like most of those in that neighbourhood, had virtually no garden or yard, but a fence in front and walls on three sides demarcated the property. The block-work of the house looked very solid, as did most of the boundary walls. However, a portion of the demarcating side boundary wall had collapsed, and lay in a heap just outside the kitchen window. Juwe explained that the wall had been damaged by the previous occupant while trying to move out. Apparently, a reversing moving van had backed into the wall and knocked down a portion of it. Juwe assured Keli and Dada that the damage would be repaired before any new occupant moved in. This house was going for Z̶Z̶75,000.

At the end of the excursion, Juwe explained that he had three other houses available, but that they were located much farther from the centre of town.

"Two of them are big mansions like the first one I showed you," he said. "The third one is a bungalow." Keli nodded.

"Maybe we can meet later this week to inspect them," Juwe continued.

"Yes, I think we should meet later in the week," said Keli. "We can discuss the houses we've already seen, or decide to look at new ones."

As Keli and Dada disembarked from the car, Juwe had some parting words:

"These houses go very fast you know, and the prices can even change from day to day. I would act quickly if I were you."

It was a unique amalgam of advice, warning and threat, which had the desired impact on the couple. They knew they had to act quickly.

Keli and Dada spent all of Sunday night evaluating the houses they had inspected. One thing was for sure: the house they would get had to be located close to the centre of Magotown. Dada was a schoolteacher and had grown accustomed to walking to her school, also located close to the town centre. There was no reliable bus service in the area, and the prospect of having to rely on expensive taxi rides to get to work did not appeal to her. Nor did the prospect of having to synchronize her official day with Keli's, so that she could ride with him to and from work. There was also the added factor of the nature of Keli's job. As a senior foreign ministry official, Keli's travels were frequent and often protracted. A house in the outlying areas would make the family feel very insecure during Keli's long absences. A house in the heart of the city would make them feel less insecure.

So, the question of inspecting Juwe's other outlying houses did not interest them. The couple's consideration was now narrowed down to the two houses inspected on Sunday afternoon. As they sat down to dinner that night, Dada opened up the topic.

"I really liked that first house we inspected. I mean the mansion."

"I like it too. So do you think we should go for it?"

"What do you think?"

"I asked you first."

Each of them may have liked the house, but neither of them really meant that they should go for it. They were merely sparring; teasing each other to see who would first admit to their inability to afford such a house.

"What about the cost?" asked Keli.

"Yes; but the man said that he could get us a loan to cover the cost."

"Yeah. And we'll spend the rest of our lives paying off the loan. That's how they entrap unsuspecting people. They sweet-talk you into taking a huge loan. They lure you into the debt trap. Once you are trapped, you become their slave and servant for ever. All your life will be spent literally working to feed their hungry appetites. Let's talk more realistically. What do you think of the second house?"

"I like it too. At least it is better than where we are living now. If we get that one, the children can have a room of their own. I pity them in their present situation where we have to force them out of their room each time we have a guest."

"So you like the second house?"

"Yes; although I wish it had a garden area where I could raise some vegetables."

"Well, it looks secure enough, and it is close enough to the shops."

"And to my school."

"And to your school."

"How much did he say it was?"

"Ẓ75,000, plus processing fees and, of course, his commission."

"Does he take a commission from us? I thought he got that from the former owners."

"I don't know about the former owners, but he told me that he takes a 5% commission from us for helping us find the house."

"And he is going to help us with the loan, too?"

"Yeah. I am told it is a package deal. And he also gets a commission for expediting the loan."

"For what?"

"Expediting the loan."

"You know what I think?" said Dada. "I think that must be jargon for the slush money he uses to bribe the loan officers. They use big grammar to hide dirty deeds."

"I don't know, and nobody is willing to say. All I know is that this is what everybody does, if they hope to stand a chance of getting the loan. Everybody in our office thinks Juwe is the right man to help us out."

"I am amazed at how much power this Juwe fellow commands."

"I am, too."

"Everybody knows he is only a mechanic. Yet he wields power over Directors and Ministers in government offices. It is amazing how a mechanic can be the wolf while a Director is the lamb."

"Yes. The presumed underdog is now the overdog."

"The whole world is upside down," added Dada.

"I think I know what gives people like Juwe influence. In his case, he's empowered by his links to the bank officials, and his detailed knowledge of what and how things could pass in the legal limbo of this struggling country. We, on the other hand, are totally vulnerable because of our relative poverty, and our unwillingness to compromise our principles."

"We have avoided using people like Juwe all these years," said Dada. "It has got us nowhere. We might as well follow the advice of your colleagues."

"I guess we have no choice."

"I regret though that we are now joining those rich-for-nothing boys at your office. Those officers are as crooked as anything you can imagine."

"I know. But we are not going to indulge in their kind of crookedness. After all the efforts we made last year, and the year before, what else can we do? Let's try Juwe and see if that is the answer to our prayers."

The matter seemed to have decided itself. The following Wednesday, Keli left the office early enough to catch Juwe at the workshop before he closed. There was a definite glint in Juwe's eye when he saw Keli.

"So you've made up your mind," he said, as Keli settled himself on a wobbly stool that passed for a visitor's chair at Juwe's workshop.

"Or did your wife make the mind up for you," Juwe added jokingly.

Keli was really in no mood for jokes.

"Incidentally," continued Juwe, "you remember the three outlying houses I said I could show you if you wanted?"

"Yes. The two mansions and a bungalow."

"Well, one of them was paid for this morning. The early bird catches the worm, you know. So you better hurry."

Again, another chuckle from Juwe. Finally, Keli spoke up.

"We don't intend to bother with those houses on the outskirts of the city."

"So, we don't have to go for inspections again today, then?" asked Juwe.

"No, we don't have to."

Juwe appeared relieved. After a full day of strenuous work, neither he nor Keli had any appetite for another house-hunting expedition.

"We are considering one of the two houses you showed us," said Keli.

"Yes?"

"You say you can help us arrange everything."

"Sure."

"Including the loan?"

"Including the loan. I've done that for dozens of people in the past couple of years."

"Okay. We're interested in the three-bedroom house."

"I thought as much."

"Yeah. We liked the big house, but I am not sure we can afford it."

"Awh!" Juwe sneered. "But you are a very senior government officer. I'm sure you can afford it if you wanted. I've seen people junior to you owning two or three such houses. Maybe you've got other things you are doing with your money."

Keli did not have other things he was doing with his money, but this was not the time or place to pursue the argument.

"The three-bedroom house," continued Juwe. "That's No. 44 Bangumba Street. Let's see…"

Juwe got up, excused himself, and went outside to his car. He returned shortly with two well-worn folders. He searched through the first folder, put it aside, then rummaged more frantically through the second folder. He returned to the first folder. "There we are!" he exclaimed as he pulled out a document from the folder. He studied it for a few seconds.

"Yes. No. 44 Bangumba Street. Beautiful house."

Keli said nothing.

"I told you it goes for ZZ75,000. That's really a give-away price."

"I take it that's the asking price," Keli said.

"Not really. We don't like to waste time bargaining and haggling, so we give you the final price right away. It's still a good buy, I can assure you."

Keli, given no choice in the matter, simply nodded in reluctant agreement. But Juwe wanted a more explicit indication of consent. "Do you still want it at that price?" he insisted.

"I guess we'll just have to take it at that."

"OK. And how big a loan will you be needing?"

Keli thought for a moment. "I figure a loan of ᵶ60,000 will be sufficient for me."

"So you have enough for the down payment."

"I think I do."

"If not, we can arrange a separate loan for that too. The interest rate for that is extremely high, but some people still take it."

"No thanks. I think I'll just stick to the main mortgage loan. ᵶ60,000 will be enough."

"I'm sure you know the fees for our services."

"Tell me."

"Well, we charge 5% of the value of the house as our finder's fee. You pay that up front, before we get down to the legal papers and the arrangements for the loan. It's a one-time payment, so you don't have to worry."

"What if I arrange my loan elsewhere?"

"Very few people do that. In any case, they still pay us for the service of helping to identify the house that they buy. It's a requirement, and it is non-refundable."

"You said you would also assist us to get the loan"

"Sure. That's part and parcel of our business. We charge 7.5% of the value of the loan for this service. We call it the loan service fee. It's also a one-time payment, but we do not insist on it until just before your loan check is given to you. You cannot get the loan money until you have paid this fee."

"How does this relate to the interest rate on the loan?"

"The interest rate is separate. That is between you and the bank. Our business is to link you with a reliable bank where you can get a good interest rate. But the actual rate is between you and them."

"Interesting."

"Yes. We try to render as much help as we can."

Keli thought over all the details for about a minute. He pulled out a piece of paper from his pocket and did some quick calculations. "OK. When do we start," he said, looking up.

"It's all up to you. As soon as I get the finder's fee, I'll know that you are serious. Then things will really start moving."

"Like what?"

"Like arranging to introduce you to the loan officer at the bank. I know him very well. So, as soon as you do your part, I'll do my part"

"Alright. I'll think about all this and get back to you in a few days."

"Fine."

The two men stood up and shook hands to seal their understanding. Juwe ushered in two of his apprentices to start locking up the premises, while he escorted Keli to his car.

Chapter 4 – Through the eye of a needle

During the ensuing weeks, Keli was held by the guiding hand of Juwe, like a child being led by the mother to negotiate a muddy passage. Together, they tip-toed through the treacherous process of home acquisition in Magotown. The first demand made on Keli was that he pay the 5% finder's fee to Juwe. This was a prerequisite for the commencement of the process. It was also Juwe's assurance that his investment of time and effort in the venture would not be in vain.

Down to the last minute, Keli was still debating whether or not he was making the right decision. First was the question of whether he should put himself in Juwe's hands and commit himself to a process that, despite the recommendations of his office colleagues, still had a large element of murkiness about it. There was always the possibility of a double-cross. Secondly, even if he stayed with Juwe, was the house at 44 Bangumba Street the best affordable one for him and his family? What if he waited a few more weeks? Something better might become available. But then again, there might be nothing better, and by then, some other eager customer would have snatched up this particular house. In that scenario, he would have great difficulty in convincing Juwe that he was a serious customer deserving of any further attention.

The night before the five percent payment was to be made to Juwe, Keli sat down with Dada to go over the prospects one more time. The gravity of the decision was amplified by the fact that a substantial part of their meagre savings was being deployed to meet this preliminary payment.

"Are you convinced that we should commit to that house - the one on Bangumba Street?" asked Keli, still feeling for the faintest trace of dithering from Dada.

"Yes. I have told you so before."

"Your mind is made up?"

"As made up as it can be. I have even taken up the habit of walking by that house on most days on my way to and from school. And each time I see it, it looks even more beautiful."

"It had better be. It is shaping up to be our dream house."

"And do you know something? The children like it, too. I took them to see it four days ago, and they seemed so delighted."

"Well, I thought I was the only one who was paying secret visits to look at that house. I have driven by it several times, just to see how it looks at various times of the day. Yesterday, I noticed that they have even started work to repair the damaged perimeter wall. "

"Yes. I noticed that, too, the day I went there with the children."

"But is Bangumba Street not too dusty and noisy for us?" asked Keli, playing the devil's advocate, and still probing for some weakness in Dada's resolve.

"Not for me. That area is just the way I like it. Not that I would reject a mansion if someone gave it to me. And not that noise and dust do any good for me. But we just have to ignore what is beyond our means, and learn to like what we can afford. That house is just fine for me, especially being so close to my school."

"Maybe when we win a lottery jackpot and become rich, we can move into a mansion. Then we can buy a second car for you to drive to work."

"That will be the day."

"I would have liked to wait a bit before committing ourselves to Juwe," said Keli. "But we don't want to risk losing that house to some more desperate person."

"That would really be a pity, especially now that we all have started to invest our emotions in this particular house. "

"Okay. Our mind is made up. Tomorrow, I will go to pay Juwe his 5% to jump-start the process."

"I am happy for us. It is going to be tough, but I am happy. A rented house is a rented house, no matter how reasonable or comfortable. Our rent payments all these years have only gone to enrich others, while sucking us dry. Now we can begin to invest in something that we can leave to our children. I am happy."

The next day, Juwe got his money, and the process started in earnest. Keli was asked to check back in a week, to see if it had been possible to secure an appointment for him at the bank. His wait was patient, but understandably anxious. If there was going to be a double-cross, this was an ideal time for it. Some money had changed hands, but no services had yet been delivered. He checked back in a week, but no appointment had yet been secured. The wait continued. Finally, about three weeks after he made his payment, Keli was invited to the bank for the transactions. Juwe escorted him there, to expedite matters.

Keli expected that most of his dealings at the bank would be with the infamous Gordon Galena, the loans manager. Keli was mistaken. Sure, Juwe took him to Gordon's office and made introductions, but they spent less than three minutes with Gordon. The shortness of the stay did not matter much though. They were soon ushered down the stairs, to the desk of a junior officer. There, elaborately laid out on the desk and in full display, were all the paraphernalia for Keli's transaction. The bank was fully prepared for Keli's visit. There were forms of all shapes, sizes and colours. Then there were brochures of different kinds. Keli filled out some of the forms on the spot, but others required information or documentation that he did not have readily at hand. Still others needed to be completed by other people, or to be signed by them. Then there were those that needed to be sworn to and notarised. In all, Keli completed three forms at the bank, and took home about a half dozen more to be completed and returned later.

The loan requested by Keli was ZZ60,000. The stipulated conditions leading up to the granting of the loan were as rigorous as the transactions were tortuous. There was nothing that the bank did not ask for: his salary slips, his tax papers, other investments if any, photocopies of his passport, his birth and marriage certificates, letters of reference, the lot. What was most irritating to Keli was that the list of required documents was not given to him in order that he could provide all the documents at once. Instead, the documents were being requested one at a time, in succession, with the provision of each document or requirement seeming to trigger a demand for yet another one.

Keli suffered through all this patiently, and in the end, all requirements were met. He paid Juwe the inscrutable "loan service fee" of 7.5% for expediting the loan. A mortgage loan of ZZ60, 000 was granted. The deal was sealed; and Keli was now the proud owner of a house of his own in Magotown. The interest rate, though flexible, was quite low at four percent, as regulated by law. The repayment period for the loan was to be twenty years. Everyone agreed that Keli had negotiated a good deal.

So it was that some nine years ago, Keli was finally able to secure a mortgage loan from the bank to buy a house. For the first four years of the loan, the interest rate remained low enough, and Keli could readily cope with the mortgage repayments. Being the disciplined civil servant that he was, Keli's mortgage repayments always reached the bank well ahead of the monthly deadlines. He was even able to put a little bit aside to commission architectural plans for his dream retirement home back in Alaku, his native village. However, in the last five years, things had become progressively more difficult. The bank, in response to inflation in the economy, had raised interest rates several times within the period. With structural adjustment and deregulation, the interest rate had sky-rocketed to 9.5%, more than double the original interest rate. The sum demanded in monthly repayment had consequently ballooned. To worsen matters, inflation in Zunguzonga had caused the cost of living to triple in the last five years. The economy, beleaguered for the past several years, was now in a state of collapse. Many local industries had shut down, and the few consumer goods that could be had were being imported from abroad. The net effect of all this was a pernicious conspiracy, which ensured that salaried people like Keli could just barely feed and clothe their families. Unfortunately, Keli's salary as Deputy Director had not increased to keep pace with the inflation in everything else. In an ironic twist, adjusting civil service salaries was always extremely difficult because of the extensive bureaucracy entailed. Civil service pay always lagged far behind the pay in other sectors of the economy. Keli was feeling the pinch and could no longer keep up with his mortgage repayments.

Keli was considered a very senior public officer, well paid in comparison to the rest of the population; with a frugal lifestyle, and no other major investments. Yet, here he was, hardly able to afford a modest house for himself and his family. The prevailing economic realities in Zunguzonga were indicating that a Deputy Director could not afford a modest three-room house. This meant that virtually every public officer of honest means was precluded from owning a house. It also meant that a large segment of the population was sentenced to a life of perpetual tenancy. Most of them were under pressure to indulge in various means, ethical or otherwise, to make extra money to afford a house.

In a curious way, the disempowerment of the middle class was a potent force that encouraged and perpetuated corruption in Zunguzonga. Many indeed had fallen victim and succumbed to the stifling temptation of official corruption. Numerous civil servants, far junior to Keli and on much lower salaries, owned strings of houses and wallowed in affluence. Nobody seemed to ask them how they came about their riches. If anything, relatives and friends were only interested in sidling up to them for whatever economic benefits could be gleaned. Indeed, many of Keli's own relatives had long subjected him to ridicule. They saw tight-fistedness in Keli, compared to the riches and benefits that other officers lavished on their relatives. But Keli was unyielding in his aversion for all forms of corruption. His family background and strict religious upbringing had given him the moral strength to resist corruption. He tried to live within his salary. This made him such a popular choice for the coveted position at the foreign ministry, where international business conglomerates were constantly scheming to compromise the unwary officer. However, this uncompromising integrity also made Keli's present predicament more intractable. While many others would have found an easy, if unethical solution, Keli was stuck. More than some others, his plight with his mortgage repayments could not find an easy remedy.

After four years of unfailing regularity, Keli's monthly repayments to the bank became less monthly. The frequency of repayments grew progressively attenuated. The irregularity lasted for nearly two years. Then, the repayments ceased altogether. For nine months, there was no repayment whatsoever.

Keli went to the bank several times for lengthy discussions during the period when his repayments became irregular. Each time, it was the same humiliating fare of supercilious bank officials contemplating the fortunes of a cowed, pleading, Keli. When he stopped repayment, he knew that such encounters would be even more humiliating, given that in the bank's court, non-payment is a more grievous crime than irregular payment. Keli was in a state of financial paralysis, and had no stomach for further humiliation. He simply stayed away from the bank, burying his head in the sand like an ostrich, while the sandstorm of financial disarray swirled all around him. His financial stupor dragged on for nine months, and was threatening to turn into a coma if left unchecked. Then fate intervened.

Chapter 5 – A striking intervention

On the second Thursday in July, Keli was having breakfast at home when he heard an unusual announcement on the radio. The secretary of the Civil Service Union announced that the CSU would be calling a press conference at noon the following day, and that some important announcements would be forthcoming. Such press conferences were quite common, but the fact that this one was presaged with such fanfare was an indication that something serious was afoot. Keli was a member of the CSU, and was quite familiar with its militancy in the pursuit of demands from government.

Keli's instincts drove him to seek more information on the announcement. On his way to work, he stopped by the newsstand and bought as many different newspapers as he could find. Sure enough, a couple of them had the announcement on the front page, but none gave any details as to what announcements might be forthcoming from the union. At the office, a message was waiting for Keli, that the minister wanted to see him. He set down his briefcase, and headed straight for the minister's office. The Honourable Minister of Foreign Affairs, not normally known for punctuality, was already in the office.

"Come in, Keli," he said. "I've been wanting to talk to you"

"Good morning, Sir."

"Yes. Sit down."

Keli settled himself into the visitors' chair. His eyes panned the ornate decorations that adorned the office walls, while the minister retrieved some documents from his desk drawer.

"Did you hear the announcement this morning?" asked the minister, going straight to the point.

"About the CSU, Sir?"

"Yes. About the CSU."

"Yes. I heard it on my radio this morning."

"Do you have any idea what it's all about?"

"No idea whatsoever. I've even scanned through the papers, but there is no clarification."

"I know you are a member of the CSU, so I will not ask you too many questions about this. In any case, we discussed the CSU demands at Cabinet last week. We must be ready for whatever they are up to."

"How do you mean 'we', Sir?"

"Yes, you senior officers must keep this place going whatever happens."

"I see, Sir. Anyway, let's hope that everything will be alright."

"We all hope so. The CSU press conference is tomorrow. Why don't we meet again here on Monday morning to assess the situation? The director will be joining us."

"Certainly, Sir."

"Meanwhile, keep your ears and eyes open, and your mouth shut."

"You know me, Sir," said Keli, as he stood up to return to his office.

Much of the corridor conversation in the offices on Thursday inevitably drifted to what the CSU might or might not do. Indeed, all of Zunguzonga was abuzz as to what the CSU might be up to this time around. Everyone hoped it was for the better, but everyone feared that the nation might be in for a period of disruptive industrial action.

Friday was the day for the CSU press conference. The venue was the Multipurpose Auditorium at the Ministry of Education. It was a relatively small auditorium, with a capacity of less than one hundred people. But it had recently been refurbished, with new ash-gray carpeting, and padded chairs to match. Ceiling fans whirled relentlessly from the high-vaulted ceilings, supplementing the struggling air conditioning system. For this occasion, the podium had two ten-foot tables placed together, with white table covers and skirting. A small bouquet of roses sat desolately on the long stretch of white, barren tabletop.

All the print and electronic media in the country were represented. The press, fully assembled as early as 11 a.m., spent the waiting period catching up with one another, or fiddling with and repeatedly testing their electronic gear. There was palpable anticipation in the air. At the scheduled press conference time of 12 noon, the CSU executive was nowhere to be seen. Fifteen minutes later, the Assistant Publicity Secretary of the union made an appearance. There was a hushed tone in the press hall as the journalists primed themselves for the conference to begin. All listened with rapt attention as the union official took the podium. But what he said was partially disappointing and partially encouraging to the gathered throng. He indicated that he had come to apologize for the lateness. The CSU executive committee meeting, at which crucial decisions were being made, was running a bit late. The press conference was still on track, but would commence at 1 p.m. The press conference, he said, would be addressed by the President of the Union, flanked by members of the executive committee.

The gathered journalists felt a bit disappointed, but none of them dared to leave. It was clear that something significant was developing, and woe to the correspondent who missed out on it. No amount of explaining to the editor back at the office would save such a correspondent from adverse consequences. All settled down and continued waiting.

At seven minutes past 1 p.m., the full executive committee of the "Civil Service (and Allied Workers) Union" breezed into the press hall. There was the president, bearded and unsmiling, wearing his customary brown beret, and holding his crowd-conjuring oxtail flywhisk. Then there was the secretary, clutching a couple of tattered-looking but fully-stuffed files. The full complement of executive committee members followed, making six union officials in all. The president sat down at the central chair, in front of the microphone, while the other officials distributed themselves on both flanks. The press conference was set to begin.

The president shook his flywhisk a couple of times at the gathered journalists, adjusted his beret, and began his address. Apparently, the lateness of the executive committee meeting had not allowed him time to write down his speech. There was no prepared text; he spoke only from hand-written notes on a piece of paper.

"You will recall that six months ago, we declared a trade dispute with the government over the salaries and work conditions of civil service workers in this country. In the intervening period, the government has not seen fit to negotiate with us in good faith. All they have done has been to employ delaying tactics and trickery in their dealings with us. Nothing, absolutely nothing, has come out of our discussions and negotiations with them.

"And what has happened to our members in the meantime? They have been reduced to a situation of utter hopelessness and poverty. As you know, there is rampant inflation in Zunguzonga today. The cost of living has been rising steeply; yet the salaries of our members have remained stagnant. Traders have raised their prices. Landlords have raised their rents. Taxis and buses have raised their fares. Even workers in the private sector have received salary increases to make up for the rise in the cost of living. We, the very people who keep the machinery of government going, are the only ones left to suffer. Yet, we have to buy from the same shops, patronize the same utilities and pay the same transport fares as everybody else"

The speaker glanced to his left, and then to his right, to make eye contact with his fellow officials who all along had been nodding in approbation. An even more vigorous nod from each CSU official recharged the president's morale to carry on.

"We are now at a point where even senior civil servants are unable to afford three square meals a day for themselves and their families. Our children are being sent home from school everyday for lack of school fees. Our landlords keep harassing us for rent, which we are unable to pay. Our salaries are delayed unnecessarily. Our leave bonuses have remained unpaid. Our relatives laugh at us as being good for nothing. It has now reached a point where something positive must be done."

He stopped speaking, and bent over to whisper something to the secretary. They whispered back and forth for about thirty seconds. At the conclusion of the *tête à tête*, the address to the journalists resumed.

"We have come up with certain positive measures designed to address this matter once and for all. We hereby give the government an ultimatum of three weeks within which to meet our demands. If our grievances are not fully satisfied in three weeks time, we and our members will consider ourselves free to take whatever action we like. We have suffered enough, and we are now ready to call the government's bluff."

The president thanked the journalists for their patience, waved the flywhisk in their direction once again, and got up to leave. But he settled back into his seat again after the dutiful secretary reminded him that they would have to answer questions from the gathered journalists.

Question time was brief, and covered only a few issues. The journalists, now running late on account of the delay in the news conference, seemed unusually eager to terminate the encounter. Some were anxious to rush off to their next assignments, while others were heading to their editorial offices to compile and file this breaking story. However, there was one point on which the few questioners pressed the CSU officials: What would happen if the government failed to meet their demands in three weeks? The president was deliberately evasive on this, and none of his union colleagues could or would clarify the matter. However, all parties were left to read between the lines. Zunguzonga might be heading towards an unprecedented and potentially devastating strike by civil service workers.

Since Zunguzonga attained independence, written and unwritten laws had proscribed trade union activity by workers in certain strategic sectors. These sectors included the army, the police, the judiciary and the civil service. They were prohibited from going on strike, or even forming unions. However, some eight years back, somebody started something called "The Civil Service Association." The government suspected that this might be a backdoor way of unionising the civil servants, and went to court to challenge the formation of the association. But the court ruled that the constitution guaranteed freedom of association, and that civil servants were entitled to those freedoms. Over the years, the Association slowly metamorphosed into the Civil Service Union, both in name and in its agenda. Everybody had come to accept the existence of the CSU, but nobody had ever seen it flex its muscles like it was doing now; and certainly nobody had ever seen a strike by civil servants in Zunguzonga. All agreed that the country was now exploring uncharted territory. Unease and uncertainty hung in the air.

As appointed, Keli met again with the minister and the director on Monday morning. He had listened to the press conference on Friday on the radio at his office, and came away with the same sense of foreboding as everybody else. Neither he nor the director was able to offer any meaningful advice to the minister. They in turn pressed the minister to tell them what the government was likely to do. The minister claimed not to know, but indicated that things would become clearer after the Minister of Labour had briefed the cabinet meeting scheduled for Monday evening. He said that he suspected that the Minister of Labour would hold a press conference within a few days of the cabinet meeting. He suggested that Keli should attend the press conference and report back to him.

The government greeted the CSU ultimatum with bravado. Three days after the ultimatum was issued, the Minister of Labour gave his own press conference. Keli, as assigned, was present. Not being a journalist, he took a seat at the outer edges of the conference hall.

The Minister of Labour began with a terse prepared statement, which he read to reporters:

"You, and indeed the whole nation, have been witnesses to the shameful ultimatum, which the so-called Civil Service Union issued to government last Friday. It is a pity that the good intentions of this government have been so crassly abused by a bunch of irresponsible, power-hungry, trade unionists. I would like to assure the nation that this Government will not be intimidated by threats or coercion from any quarters.

"We are committed to the improvement of the conditions of all workers in this country, within the limits of our financial resources. We recognize the very crucial importance of the civil servants of this nation, and will spare no effort to improve their situation. The government team that has been negotiating with them has been reorganized and revitalized, and is ready to resume serious negotiations. Meanwhile, let no one be left in doubt about our resolve to maintain the rule of law in this country. Groups that commit or promote illegal acts will need to justify their continued existence to the people of this country. A word is enough for the wise."

The minister concluded his statement, gathered up his files, and left the room without entertaining any questions. Keli remained in his seat until the hall was nearly empty. He found the minister's tense demeanour and abrupt departure every bit as dramatic as the press conference show that the CSU officials had put on three days earlier.

The minister's uncompromising stance and implied threats did not go down well with the CSU officials. The three-week ultimatum period began to tick away. Given the hardening of positions on both sides, very few people expected a resolution of the issues within the three-week period. The best that could be hoped for was the resumption of meaningful negotiations before the period elapsed. In the end, even this more modest goal was only barely achieved. The negotiating parties got to work some 15 days after the ultimatum was issued. At this stage, each side was eager to save face, and realized that they needed the other side to help them do so. There appeared to be a renewed eagerness for compromise. The negotiations were progressing well, and both sides issued hopeful public statements. So, when the ultimatum deadline came, it was conveniently ignored by the CSU, in the expectation that the issue would soon be resolved. Negotiations continued.

Two weeks after the ultimatum deadline, the government announced the reconstitution of the boards of several government-owned (i.e. parastatal) companies and commissions. This reconstitution had been in the making for three months, and was part of a routine annual reorganization of parastatal boards by the government. Among various new board appointments, the secretary of the CSU was appointed to the board of the Energy Regulation Commission. The government saw this appointment as a way of extending a hand of friendship to the CSU. The CSU secretary saw it the same way, and had written back to the government to accept the appointment. But the CSU rank and file did not see it that way. They saw it as a veiled attempt by government to bribe their union officials into submission, and thereby weaken their struggle for better conditions. Within days, demonstrations were organized demanding that the government should withdraw the appointment, and that the secretary should not accept. With his integrity and future career now squarely on the line, it did not take much for the secretary to issue a public statement declining the appointment. Of course, he did not let it be known to his supporters that he had earlier accepted the offer. He quietly wrote a letter to the government, withdrawing his earlier letter of acceptance. With this minor hiccup resolved, all attention was again refocused on the on-going negotiations.

Some issues appeared relatively easy to resolve, and were deliberately tackled first. This helped to build confidence between the two sides. It was not difficult to reach agreement on such matters as the reviewing of civil service salaries every three years, the rate at which leave bonuses should be paid, and the improvement of promotion prospects. As the negotiations moved on to more contentious issues, traction became more difficult. The government side claimed that civil servants had been unproductive, and deserved only a modest increase in salaries. The union countered that civil servants were no more and no less productive than their counterparts in the private sector, and therefore deserved equivalent levels of remuneration. Amity slowly gave way to suspicion, and eventually, stalemate. Hard-earned confidence, built at the earlier stages, began to erode at its foundation. It tottered, and then, finally collapsed. The negotiations broke down. The CSU officials packed up their files and left, threatening dire consequences for what they described as the government's insensitivity to the plight of the common people.

The threat was not for nothing. Three days after the negotiations broke down, the CSU announced that its members were embarking on an indefinite strike, effective immediately. The strike would not end until the contentious issues between the CSU and the government were resolved.

Civil servants throughout the country dutifully obeyed their union's call. They had been following the negotiations very closely, and waited with keen expectation for the improved salaries and conditions that might result. Now that the negotiations had broken down, they agreed fully with the CSU that the government needed additional pressure if meaningful concessions were to be extracted from it. Nobody, except perhaps the government, bothered about the legality or otherwise of a civil service strike. It had never been done before, and no one could predict what impact it might have on the nation.

The strike started quite abruptly, and its impact was immediate. Government business was paralysed and chaos reigned throughout the country. Any aspect of life that depended directly or indirectly on government services was crippled or shut down. And in Zunguzonga, that meant almost everything. Even the courts and some parastatals had to shut down when their normal retinue of supporting civil service staff failed to show up for work. The effect of the strike also spilled over into the private sector. Some private businesses stagnated due to inability to process licences, certificates and other regulatory documentation from government offices. All told, the strangling effect of the strike far exceeded the expectations of the CSU officials. Their snare was slowly but surely eroding the government's position. CSU members sat in the corner, wringing their hands and waiting for a crack in the government's resolve. It did not take long.

One week into the strike, and with mounting public unease at its effects, cowed government officials sent out feelers to the CSU for the resumption of negotiations. They asked the CSU to call off the strike so that negotiations could resume in a less charged atmosphere. The CSU agreed to resume negotiations, but on the condition that it would leave the strike in place while negotiations continued. The strike would only be called off after the issues in dispute had been agreed on. The CSU knew that the strike was its most potent weapon. They would not easily give it up. Both sides were now playing to the gallery of public opinion, and neither side wanted to be blamed for the suffering, which the strike was now wreaking on the daily lives of ordinary people. In the face of CSU's insistence, the government agreed to resume negotiations while the strike dragged on.

The strike provided a crisis background under which this new bout of negotiations was conducted. It also showed both sides what the unpalatable default position would be if the negotiations should fail again. Therefore, all delegates to the negotiation sessions approached this round in a very businesslike manner. The nation was waiting for the results of their efforts to lift the yoke of the strike from its shoulders.

For most of the striking civil servants, the period of the strike was spent in relative idleness. Some used it to catch up on long-postponed private obligations. Others travelled to their villages to help out with farm work; while still others were able to secure informal part-time jobs in the city.

For Keli, the strike presented a completely different prospect. The period was not spent in relative idleness at all. If anything, a curious set of circumstances conspired to make this period a living hell for him. Although technically a member of the CSU, Keli was seen in practice as very senior. Like it or not, he was seen as part of the management team that had to maintain skeletal government services during the strike. And such skeletal services were particularly imperative at the Foreign Ministry where a façade of normalcy had to be maintained to protect the country's image. It would nearly be tantamount to treason for Keli to abandon his Atlas-like position just because of the strike. Patriotic instincts therefore dictated that Keli had to stay on the job. Worse still, he had to do his work without the support of the usual retinue of assistants and aides to which he was accustomed. There were no secretaries, no clerks, no messengers, no assistant directors; virtually nobody. He found himself saddled with an unimaginable array of office tasks, which would normally have been performed by his striking subordinates. Most of these were tasks that he had outgrown many years back. Each day, he worked from morning until well into the night trying to keep up with the essential duties and tasks that had to be performed. While everybody else around him was in a semi-vacation mode, Keli was constrained to be in an emergency work overload mode. He dreaded each day, and looked forward anxiously to the end of the strike.

Six weeks after the strike began, the CSU announced that agreement had been reached with government on all the major issues. The strike was being called off. Zunguzonga breathed a huge sigh of relief, and prepared itself to start undoing the damage that had been inflicted on it by the protracted strike. Civil servants, now weary of the imposed idleness, were only too happy to be back at work again. They dusted up their idle desks, spruced up their offices, opened up long-dormant files, and the nation was in business once again. The corridors of power that had for so long been silent, once again resonated with the sounds of pounding feet and human laughter. Government offices once more bustled with their usual bureaucratic activity.

Chapter 6 – I'm in a debt trap, so is my country

The end of the civil service strike brought double relief to Keli. Only too happy to be relieved of the feeling that the fate of the nation rested on his shoulders, he could now return to his normal workload, and have his aides available to assist him. He also felt that the CSU had negotiated astutely. The end of the strike ushered in a substantial salary increase for all civil servants. Keli got a reasonable salary increase, plus a huge lump sum in salary arrears. Things were looking up. He could now lift his head from the figurative sand of financial stupor, and contemplate getting in touch with his mortgage bank.

He did just that, uncertain of what he might find. Even though the total amount already repaid now exceeded the value of the original loan, the amount of indebtedness remaining in Keli's mortgage account was still quite substantial. The ballooning interest rates, and compounding of unpaid arrears, ensured that the figures kept multiplying. Such is the magic of bank loans and compound interest, that borrowers sometimes have to pay the value of the loan several times over before they finally get out of it. With his economic situation now improved, Keli's mortgage repayment machine once again spurted into action, after a one-year hiatus. The machine picked up steam and held steady for some months. Soon, it began to feel the strain again and began to labour. It sputtered for a few more months. Then, it gave up in exhaustion. Finally.

The bank was observing Keli's discomfiture with a mixture of displeasure and anxiety. They would like to stretch out the period of Keli's indebtedness, and of their interest receipts, to as many years as possible. After all, the bank was dependent on such interest payments for its own survival. That was exactly what they were in the business for. So, the longer Keli or anybody else was indebted to them, the better. It suited them just fine if Keli was indebted to them for all of his lifetime, so long as he kept on servicing the debt with frequent repayments. Moreover, with re-scheduling of the loan, compounding of the unpaid interest, and extending the repayment period at Keli's request, the bank had reasonable assurance that Keli had been securely ensnared and enslaved in their debt trap. All that was needed now was to ensure that he survived enough to continue to repay, but did not thrive enough to pay off the debt and buy his freedom. Surviving, but not thriving; that was the formula.

This formula was not totally unknown to Keli. From his years at the foreign ministry, he had seen a similar phenomenon operate at the international level, where debt traps feature just as prominently as in personal financial affairs. A good example was an event held about six months after the infamous civil service strike ended. It was a special seminar for senior officials in Keli's ministry. The main topic of discussion was foreign aid, with a special emphasis on foreign debts. The director at the foreign ministry had the responsibility of presenting the plenary paper around which the discussion sessions would be built. But the director was busy preparing for a foreign trip with the minister. He delegated the responsibility for the seminar paper to Keli, which also meant that Keli had to lead the follow-up discussion sessions. Keli silently resented the extra work that his boss had dumped on him; but saw the seminar as an opportunity to give vent to some issues that had agitated his mind for years.

He prepared the main paper, and then printed out a summary, which he photocopied and distributed to participants. After an introductory paragraph, the summary read:

"The paper laments how the politicians have incurred huge debts for the country, goaded on by the phantom of rapid development and innocuous-looking loans from developed countries. While many of the projects that attracted the loans have failed or never even got off the ground, the resulting indebtedness remains robust and flourishing. In many cases, the only lasting edifice left from the projects is the monumental debt staring the country in the face. This monument is like a caged monster that has to be continually fed to keep it happy and prevent it

from devouring its minders. It is well known that the country is now spending more on servicing foreign debt, than on current development efforts. Current resources that could be used to improve the lot of the poor, are being delivered to the rich nations as debt repayment. With the country's economy perpetually in a coma, there is little prospect that the debts could be decreased, and absolutely no prospect that the debts could be liquidated. The main remedy being offered by the creditors seems to be additional loans, which, insidiously, would only oil the springs in the debt trap and make them stronger. This means that the fate of future generations has effectively been compromised; mortgaged; auctioned. All efforts towards genuine development will be like swimming against a tide with the millstone of debt repayment tied around the neck."

Keli delivered the paper with as much vehemence as he had packed into the distributed summary. He was loudly applauded by the audience, which consisted of other civil servants, a few business people, and a sprinkling of political appointees. However, the critical tone of the paper towards politicians did not escape attention. There were several probing questions when he finished his presentation. Mr. Tolo Folo, the ubiquitous political adviser to the minister was, of course, present, and was particularly keen to understand where Keli stood. When it was indicated that the floor was open for discussion and questions, Tolo was the first to speak.

"So, are you saying that the international creditors are to blame for our poor state of development?" he asked Keli.

"Yes, and no," was the answer.

"How do you mean?"

"First, let us talk about the international financial bodies whom you have referred to. They come in here, claiming to know everything. They claim to know more about us than we do about ourselves. And they claim to have the medicine that can cure all."

"But more often than not, their financial medicine does not work," added Tolo.

"Yes. When their medicine fails, they turn around and blame you," Keli continued. "They say that the fundamentals of their prescription were right; only that the environment in which you were implementing the prescription was not right. But did they not know about that environment in the first place? Why did they not factor it into their calculations, so as to give us a prescription that can work in our socio-cultural environment? Just because a formula works in their own country, they go around forcing the same panacea on everybody else."

"I grew up on a farm," volunteered Tolo, "so let me give you an analogy from the farm. It is something like this. Let's say I am currently growing a crop variety that germinates well on my soil, but only yields three tonnes per hectare. You yourself have another variety of the crop that germinates well on your soil, and yields twenty tonnes per hectare. You notice the difference. Then without testing your seed on my soil, you come over and pressure me to abandon my variety and accept yours. But alas; too late we both find out that your variety is unable to even germinate on my soil, much less grow. So, there is no opportunity to realize the huge yield potential. We can only say that your seed is better for me if the entire package works, from germination to harvest. If your high-potential seed cannot even germinate in my environment, then the entire package is a failure, and I am better off if I had never been pressured to abandon my previous low-yielding seed. That is the way I see these international financial institutions. Look at how many nations that have had their economies crumble under the weight of the restructuring prescriptions from these international bodies. Many nations are worse off than they were at the onset. It's a great pity."

"You would think," suggested Keli, "that some of these institutions are much smarter than that; but maybe their actions are driven by their own economic and political calculations. It may be a case of the international financial institutions blatantly protecting the interests of those who provide money for their operations. I guess there may be some equity in that. He who pays the piper dictates the tune. In that case though, they should not pretend to the world that the piper's financiers are not calling the tune. They should come out plainly and say so, rather than laying sanctimonious claims to ethical purity. I certainly lament the fate of our country under the supercilious gaze of the international creditors."

The discussion session was supposed to involve the entire audience; but it was threatening to turn into a dialogue between Tolo and Keli. Finally, the monotony was broken. A middle-aged lady sitting near the aisle was recognized to make her contribution. The microphone was passed over to her.

"I can see that I am one of the few women in this audience," she began, as she panned her bespectacled eyes over the seated gathering. "So, I will talk about an aspect of foreign aid that some of you men may not fully appreciate. I will comment on the question of food aid. Three years ago, the price of rice and other foodstuffs was very low, and even poor people like me could afford three square meals. Do you know why the price was low? Because plenty of food was coming in as food aid from the developed countries, as well as massive food importation by business people. All kinds of exotic foods were available here. There was plentiful supply, and the people were happy. But since the present government came into office, they have adopted a policy of discouraging food aid, and even discouraging the importation of food. Now, the supply of food is very low, and the prices are very high. We are forced to eat locally produced things that would not normally be our first choice, given the altered appetite that our children now have. We are deprived of all those nice foods that people in other parts of the world are eating. All of us are suffering and there is bitterness. Can anybody tell me why we should not restore food aid and food importation for our country, so that food will become cheap and abundant as before?"

There was scattered applause in the gathering as the woman concluded her contribution. The question had to be addressed. Being the principal speaker, Keli could not evade the responsibility. He began diffidently.

"As you know, policy is made by the government, and not by civil servants like me. I am only there to give advice. At any rate, the question of foreign aid in the form of food is a very tricky one. On the plus side, as you have said, food aid has the effect of making food plentifully available and cheap. This is politically popular with the masses especially in the cities. Many politicians like food aid because it gives the people cheap food and keeps them happy. That is always good for a few extra votes. But have you thought of the effect of food aid on local food producers? It has a devastating effect on them. Consumers turn their backs on the locally produced food, and the local food industry regresses. Entrepreneurs are reluctant to invest in local food production for fear of losing their money. In the long run, food aid has the effect of killing off local food production. It is a short-term solution that produces a long-term problem. A similar thing happens when the food is imported through commercial channels outside the food aid program. Even when you factor in transportation costs, such food often reaches here cheaper than the cost at which our local producers can produce it. This is why you find that locally produced rice and other grains are more costly than imported ones. Go to the local markets and see…"

Tolo's hand shut up in the air, seeking immediate recognition to speak. Without waiting to be acknowledged, he was already on his feet.

"This last point you made really baffles me. A consignment of grains is produced overseas thousands of kilometres away; they process it; they store it; they transport it over the oceans; they offload it; re-pack it and distribute it. And you say that after paying all those costs, the grain still sells cheaper in the store here than the one grown and produced two kilometres down the road. What gives rise to this situation? Is it because our farmers are so inefficient?"

Keli replied, "The inefficiency in the production systems of our farmers is a major factor. We lack facilities and inputs to match those of the developed countries. So, our production costs are higher. But there is another factor, a less visible one. What most people do not know is that the food that we import from the developed countries is highly subsidized. So, some of the food arrives here selling for prices below the production costs. For many of the developed countries, paying subsidies to farmers has gone on for generations, and is unlikely to stop soon. For some of them, it would be political suicide to stop the subsidy programs. So, with the double punch of subsidized foreign food and less efficient production, our farmers are at a double disadvantage."

A gentleman wearing a brown coat in the corner was recognized to contribute to the discussion.

"If the developed countries are maintaining farmer subsidies," he asked, "why has our government recently been so insistent on removing farmer subsidies here?"

"Well," answered Keli, "the plain truth is that some of these countries that subsidize their own farmers are the very ones pressuring us to remove the subsidies for our farmers. They even place the removal of subsidies as a pre-condition for granting us loans or aid. They call it "re-structuring". We are being pressured to do what they cannot do in their own systems. Yes; such is the hypocrisy of international politics."

There was a lull in the proceedings. All raised hands had been recognized to speak. The gathering had run out of persons wishing to contribute, and it looked as if the session would wind up. Suddenly, the session came alive again with a question from Tolo.

"We have talked at length about the foreigners, and their part in our plight. What do you have to say about our own people?"

This was a tricky question, especially coming from the political adviser to the minister. Keli was aware of the need to choose his words carefully in crafting an answer.

"Our own people are equally guilty," replied Keli, after a brief pause to gather his thoughts. "It is our own people that keep the door open for the international bodies to come and mess around with us. It is we who create the problems in the first place, thereby necessitating international intervention. Look at the disarray that we are in right now. How could successive leaders of our nation have been so inept, so banal, and so venal, that they allowed our country to drift into such a sorry state?"

Keli's question hung in the hushed air of the silent auditorium. The question was not answered, but the point was made. The seminar could not escape the conclusion: that complicity and culpability for the international debt trap were shared between local and international players.

Keli was certainly well versed in the intricacies of the international debt trap. Where he lacked previous experience was in the equally insidious area of the personal debt trap. Lately though, he was making up for the deficit. He was getting a painful crash course in the personal debt trap, thanks to his travails with the mortgage bank.

But what happens when a compliant slave refuses to work and be productive to justify his keep? He becomes a liability, an embarrassment, and a loss leader for the owner. That was precisely the bank's feeling when Keli's repayments stopped again. With increasing apprehension and frustration at the situation, the bank felt that it had no choice but to act. Three months into the latest default period, a warning letter was sent to Keli. There was no response. The ostrich's head had resumed its position deep in the sand. Two months later, another warning letter. Still no response. Then a final notice from the bank that it might have to foreclose and sell the house to recover the debt.

After waiting for another four months, the bank issued the same final warning again. This time, the letter was registered, so Keli had to go to the post office to pick it up and sign for it. As he opened and read it hurriedly in the post office corridor, his heart sank with despair and anxiety. He hurried home to share the threatening news with Dada.

"Achoo! These people are after us again," he announced to Dada almost as soon as he stepped inside the house

"Which people?"

"The mortgage bank. They are threatening us again."

He slipped the letter into Dada's hands, and they both slumped into separate chairs in the living room. Dada studied the letter for a couple of minutes, and then uttered a long poignant sigh, her equivalent of unspoken ululation. Then, silence for several minutes.

"What do you think we should do?" Dada broke the silence.

"I don't really know. I still like this house, and will do anything to try to save it."

"Me, too. Do you think they will really try to take it from us?"

"I don't know. All I know is that they have an uphill task ahead of them," added Keli, mustering some courage. "You remember my cousin Pali. He has been receiving such final warnings from his bank for over three years now; but somehow he has managed to keep his bank at bay. If Pali can do it, we can do it too. I am sure that will give us plenty of time to rectify matters."

"Of course, you know Pali is a smooth talker. And he has a lot of connections," Dada said

"We may not have the connections like Pali, but the law is on our side. The process of foreclosure is not easy you know. It is very lengthy. It requires legal notice by them, advertisement in the media, and eventually public auction. Such a process can take months, if not years. And, we could always stop the process at any stage if we manage to put forward a reasonable sum towards repayment of our loan."

"We sure could use the breathing space."

"Even if matters came to a head and this house has to be sold, do you know how much a house like this could be worth now? You keep complaining about the inflation in the economy, and how the prices of foodstuffs and housekeeping items have sky-rocketed. Well, the inflation is not confined to household items. It has impacted property prices as well. I estimate that a house like ours is now worth about Z̶Z̶300,000. That's about four times what we paid for it."

"So?"

"So, if they decide to take it and auction it, the proceeds will be enough to pay off our debt to the bank. It may even leave extra money, which we can use to lay the foundation for our long-contemplated house in our home village. I am not advocating that we sit idly and let them take the house. I am simply trying to see the silver lining in the cloud, if the worst should happen."

"God forbid!"

"Don't worry, DD. We've got time."

They have had five months of expectant quiet since that registered, final letter. Now, the visit by Mr. Skoop with his lawyer was stirring things up in a most unexpected and unpleasant way.

Chapter 7 – Going home to recharge

After Keli's bravado in the encounter with Mr. Skoop and his lawyer, more sober reflection set in. His leave-time peace had been so rudely disturbed, and his restless mind kept replaying the incident. Could it be true that he had forfeited his house? Could it be a joke? Could it be an attempt at fraud? Could it be a case of mistaken identity or mistaken documentation? In the end, he was inclined to dismiss it all as a crass practical joke. After all, he was sufficiently versed in the regulations to know that the process of forfeiture was a lengthy one. But Dada was not so sure.

"There are so many corrupt people around these days, you know," she argued. "Hard times have turned a lot of people into fraudsters. There is no limit to what they can do."

"So you think I should take those jokers seriously?" asked Keli

"Yes. You never know about these things."

"DD, I know how you are always fretting. I am not as convinced as you are, but I will try to ask around

65

just to make sure. I have plenty of time now that I am on leave. Once I resume duty in a few weeks, I am scheduled for a lengthy foreign trip with the minister, and the sheer pressure of work will leave me little time."

"Yes, we better look into the matter now."

"How do you suggest I should go about it?"

"I think we need advice. And not just from anybody who might turn out to be a fraudster as well. Good, solid, trusted advice."

Keli knew what that meant. For unadulterated good advice, Keli invariably turned to his relatives and friends in Alaku, his home village.

"So you think I should travel home?' he enquired of Dada

"At least you can get the wisdom of the elders. And their blessing too, for this battle that we are fighting alone. It is never good to fight alone. We need their spiritual support."

Keli had no counter argument. He had planned all along to spend a few days of the leave in the peace and quiet of Alaku, but had intended to make the trip a couple of weeks later. Peace and quiet were now far from him in any setting. He agreed with Dada that he should leave for Alaku as soon as possible.

Two days after Mr. Skoop's unforgettable visit, Keli left for Alaku, accompanied by his eight-year old son, Bedemu. Bedemu was the oldest of Keli's three children. He was born slightly premature at the Magotown General Hospital. Despite a few anxious days immediately following his birth, he recovered rapidly and developed normally, thanks mainly to the good medical attention at the nation's best hospital. Had he been born in Alaku or one of the provincial health centres, the outcome might have been much less desirable. He grew up to be his father's best friend. Indeed, Bedemu was everybody's best friend. He was extremely brilliant for his age, and his curiosity knew no bounds. Yet, he was very polite, caring, and gentle, especially in his dealings with his younger siblings. His high intelligence was already manifesting itself at school, where he consistently came among the top three in his class. His gentle ways made him popular among his classmates. They often called him by the nickname "banana boy", a reflection of his avid liking for that particular fruit.

The fondness between the Bedemu and his father was manifested in the frequency with which Bedemu accompanied him on trips or errands. This trip home was no exception. Both loaded their luggage into Keli's cranky old car, and headed first for Magotown's shopping district on Wewak Street. Having bought sundry gifts for the people at home, and a few things for themselves, they embarked on a tedious four-hour journey over some of the roughest roads on earth. Bedemu was bubbling with the excitement of going home again, and kept up the chattering for the first couple of hours. Half way through the trip, his excitement overwhelmed him, and he dozed off. He slept for the rest of the trip.

It was already getting dark when they got to the village. Alaku was a small rural village, tucked away in the western part of Zunguzonga. A narrow, sandy unpaved road ran through the village in a north-south direction. Houses of all sorts were arrayed on both sides of this road: brick-walled houses with corrugated sheet roofing, mud houses with thatched roofing, and a couple of storied buildings. Water erosion was a constant menace on this main road, and the village frequently raised communal workgroups to keep the road in reasonable repair. The only educational institution in the village, the Alaku Primary School, was also located along this road. Smaller barely-motorable secondary streets branched from the main road, meandering and attenuating until they found the edge of the forest or transformed into narrow bush paths that led to the farms.

Subsistence agriculture was the main economic activity in Alaku. There was no electricity or pipe-borne water, so the ability of small-scale industries to take root was very limited. Yet, the people of Alaku lived relatively happy lives, contenting themselves with the unending cycle of village festivals and ceremonies.

Arriving Alaku at dusk, or after it, suited Keli just fine, since it permitted him to slip into the village without attracting much attention. In contrast, arriving during daylight hours would alert the entire village of his presence, and trigger an unending stream of welcome and unwelcome visitors. Most of the visitors were well-meaning, but a good number of them came with the thinly-disguised motive of squeezing yet another gift or stipend out of a financially strapped Keli. The lives and tales of the village folk were miserable enough, and only the most hard-hearted soul could resist offering some material help to ameliorate their misery.

But there was one visitor Keli did not mind receiving, and to whom he sent word shortly after arriving at the village. Okolo Ibeme was the deputy headmaster at the village primary school. He and Keli attended that same school several decades earlier. While Keli's career had led him on a more cosmopolitan course, Okolo never strayed far from the village, departing only briefly for his training as a teacher. He was the oldest of four children, but they had lost their father while they were still young, forcing Okolo at an early age to begin to provide emotional support as a surrogate father for his siblings. Unlike Keli, Okolo married early, and was the proud father of three sons.

Teaching was Okolo's main job, but he was also an avid farmer, angler and hunter. The hours after school, and all of his weekends, were devoted to these subsidiary pursuits which, incidentally, supplemented his meagre income as a teacher. He was a strong believer in traditional village values, and ensured that his three young sons were already skilled in the traditional professions of farming and hunting. He lived frugally, and took an active interest in the cultural life of Alaku.

Okolo was only three months older than Keli. They were classmates in the several years of primary schooling that they did in Alaku. Even though Okolo and Keli hardly ever lived in the same community since their childhood parting, they remained extremely close in spirit. Each one inevitably consulted the other in matters of substance, or in times of crisis. More important, each one had an absolute respect for the other. Keli respected Okolo's innate instincts, and his deep knowledge of village traditions and nuances. Okolo in turn respected Keli's learnedness, and his experience in matters of the world beyond the village. Together, they made a complementary pair. They were friends.

Despite his sagacity and official status in the city, Keli was still regarded as a boy in this most traditional of villages. After all, his father was still alive, as were most of his uncles, not to mention his maternal grandmother. In a society where age was perhaps the dominant factor in social positioning, Keli's relative youth placed him very far down in the pecking order. His behaviour, attire and patterns of addressing people all had to show that he recognized his subordinate boyish position. The world of the village was indeed totally different from the world of the city. Keli, every bit a man in the city, was always a boy in the village. His life consisted of constantly juggling the conflicting requirements of both worlds.

Further accentuating Keli's puerile status in Alaku was the fact that he was yet to erect a house of his own in the village. Erecting a house was the ultimate manifestation of manhood among his people; and Keli was yet to discharge this obligation. To his people, a house in the village was almost like a phallic symbol whose erection was a public demonstration of virility. The size of the house did not matter, so long it was clearly identified as belonging to Keli. Indeed, his own father's house was extremely small, little more than a hut; but it served the symbolic purpose and had sufficed for the immediate family since Keli's childhood. In recent years, the smallness of the house had begun to prove embarrassingly suffocating to Keli each time he and his family visited home. Fortunately, his rich cousin, Pali, had room to spare in his house next door. So, for the past couple of years, Keli's home visits saw him occupying a spare room at Pali's. Bedemu, on the other hand, usually opted to stay in the small family house, where he could enjoy the maximum attention of his doting grandfather.

Ojiso, Keli's father, was in his early sixties. A mild encounter with polio in his childhood had left him with a slight limp in his left leg. Fortunately, the limp was slight enough to permit him all the normal physical activities of village life. His heavily furrowed brow and wrinkled cheeks bore ample evidence of a hard life spent eking out a living in Alaku. An old man by village standards, he had lived in Alaku all his life, travelled very little, and was basically a subsistence farmer. Ojiso was very fond of children. He waited a long time for a grandchild. That prayer was answered with the birth of Bedemu, with whom he developed an intensely positive interactive chemistry.

Keli's traditional obligation to build a house in the village was not considered as discharged even when he acquired his now-contentious house in Magotown. It would not be discharged even if he acquired a hundred houses in the city, contentious or not. A house in the village was a totem of manhood, and possessed a unique traditional significance. Partly for this reason, land for erecting the village house was usually given to natives of the village free of charge, from the communal lands. The same applied to Keli. Following persistent pleas by well-meaning villagers that their illustrious son should be offered a place to erect his village house, Keli had, almost reluctantly, acquired one such piece of land; free of charge. That had been nearly a decade ago. But Keli's finances had not permitted him to begin construction; and many village onlookers were beginning to whisper about the inactivity. Apart from a few heaps of sand and gravel on the plot, there was little indication of imminent development activity.

Okolo was not very surprised when he got the message that Keli was around. He knew that Keli was on leave, and had expected him to visit Alaku sometime during the leave. The only element of surprise was that Keli had showed up much earlier in the leave period than Okolo had been led to believe. All the same, it was good news. Okolo needed no further prompting.

By nine o'clock the same evening, Okolo's knock on the door roused Keli from the easy chair on which he was sprawled out, resting. Hilarious greetings were exchanged as the two friends squeezed each other in warm embrace. They soon settled into seats. Traditional refreshments were produced, and the boyhood jokes began to fly.

"I am happy that you sent for me," said Okolo.

"I did not send for you."

"Yes, you did."

"Achoo! Don't get me in trouble. How could I have sent for you when I know that you are older than I am. I have not forgotten that in Alaku, a younger person should always go to the older person, not the other way around. I recognize that it is considered an insult for a young one to send for an older one. Don't think that you are the only one who remembers our traditions."

"So, if you did not send for me, what did you do then?"

"My message was simply to inform you that I had arrived; not to summon you."

"Well, I am glad to see that you still recognize the importance of age in our traditional society."

"Yes, I do. There must be some good reasons why our ancestors placed so much emphasis on age as a social factor."

"What do you think the reasons were?"

"I don't know for sure, but I have often thought about the matter. You know that in the time of our ancestors, infant mortality was high, and life expectancy was generally short. Surviving each year of life was a battle. So, anyone who lived to anything close to old age, indeed had a victory worth celebrating. It was a status worth flaunting. Those who had not yet attained a certain age had every cause to defer to those who had, given the high probability that they themselves might not live that long."

"I think there was another reason why they made age such an important social criterion," interjected Okolo.

"What?"

"Age is very peculiar. It creates a difference that is permanent and immutable. You can be shorter than your friend today, and taller than him tomorrow. You can be fatter than him today, and thinner tomorrow. You can be poorer than him today, and richer tomorrow. The same can be said of health, education and most of life's characteristics. But once you are older than your friend, even by one day, there is no possible way in your lifetimes for him to make up the difference. Just as you have been struggling all your life to catch up on the three months head start that I have on you."

"I know I'll never catch up."

"Yeah. It sounds strange, but in a sense, age brings all social classes to the same level. Age is determined by nature, and defies human intervention or manipulation. Tamper-proof, you might say. Here in Alaku, age is seen as a God-given status symbol that attracts respect and adulation. You people in the cities and western societies are all too anxious to show how young you are. By contrast, we traditional village people are ever eager to assert our age over others, and to expect the resulting respect and deference due to an older person."

"Yes. In Alaku, age is everything. Very old people are seen as the seat of wisdom."

"They are also our spiritual links to the ancestors," added Okolo.

The jovial mood continued, as the two friends warmed up to each other.

"There is a joke I have been saving for you for the last few weeks," said Keli.

"Oh no. Not one of your dirty jokes."

"Not a dirty one this time, but an embarrassing one. I think it's very funny."

"Funny?"

"Yes. And the joke was on me."

"Ah! If it was on you, it must have been very funny."

"Very funny indeed. Especially since this is something that actually happened."

"OK. Tell me. I'm all ears."

"Well, it happened about a month ago, just before I started my leave. We were holding one of our quarterly meetings where senior officers from the various ministries get together to iron out and coordinate issues."

"The Inter-ministerial Board meetings you always talk about?"

"Yes. That's what we call them. The Head of the Civil Service was there as chairman. My Director was there. All the other Directors from various ministries were there, in this big committee room. As the meeting struggled through its lengthy agenda, things became really boring. We had been on for most of the day, and were now inching our way towards the tail end of the agenda. The matters under discussion were routine, though time-consuming. Somehow, I felt it would be rude of me to abandon the meeting and leave, especially because most of the distinguished Board members were still there, labouring under the weight of the tedium. I was obliged to sit through the drudgery of the long-drawn-out meeting.

"My mind kept drifting between the meeting and other things. I doodled on every piece of paper in front of me, and then some. Finally, in a reflex fit of boredom, I fell prey to an act which I had learned not to perform in public since our primary school days here in Alaku. I picked my nose. Yes. I picked my nose. The picking was brief, lasting less than a second; but it had encountered a flake in the inner recesses of the left nostril. Worse still, it had dislodged the flake, and I could not immediately locate where the flake had been dislodged unto. I feared the worst. Maybe the flake of dried phlegm was now perched precariously on my moustache, and making me look totally unpresentable to the distinguished company all around me. Or could the flake have fallen innocuously and unnoticed into the pile of agenda papers in front of me?

"I was taking no chances. The errant flake had to be sought out, and its embarrassment potential defused. First, I discreetly checked the nostril again to make sure the flake was not still there. It was not. Then I ran my finger several times through my bushy moustache, in an attempt to locate the flake. It was not there either, but in the absence of a mirror, I could not be sure. I ran my fingers furiously again through the moustache, this time not aiming to locate the flake, but instead aiming to vigorously wrest it from its perch, if indeed it had perched. In belated mindfulness of acceptable manners, out came my handkerchief. I scoured the left nostril with it, and for good measure, the other nostril as well. Then I gave the moustache and upper lip a thorough going over. With each wipe, I would check the handkerchief to see if I had succeeded in reining in the mysterious flake. Perhaps I had succeeded, but there was no visual assurance of that.

"At this stage, I was beginning to lose my composure. Certainly, I was no longer following the Board's deliberations. All I could think about was that everyone in the room was casting glances at me and wondering why I had a flake of phlegm on my moustache. Overcome by the uncertainty, I finally rose from my seat. After the usual perfunctory bow to the Chair, I left the room.

"I dashed straight for the toilet, with its large all-revealing mirror. There, in the privacy of the enclosure, I could finally see my public face, moustache and all. To my utter reassurance, there was no flake on my moustache, on my nostril, or on any other part of my face.

"I returned to the meeting room, triumphant in the assurance that my face was looking its normal decent self. My composure returned, but my concentration on the Board's deliberations did not return fully. For the rest of the meeting, I kept wondering where on earth the crazy flake had disappeared to. Could it have fallen to the ground in the first place and been inadvertently trodden under foot by me? Or could it have been perched victoriously on my agenda papers, mockingly witnessing my frantic search for it? I am not sure who the ultimate loser was in this encounter: was it the flake, myself, or the Board meeting? I have learned my lesson, though. When it comes to the itchy nose, the wisest thing is to leave good enough alone. At least in public."

"Sure. That will teach you," said Okolo, barely catching his breath from the fit of laughter that had seized him shortly after Keli's narration started. "Shame on you. Finger in your nose. Tortured by a phlegmatic flake of phlegm. It serves you right. What do you expect Bedemu and others to do, if you are still picking your nose at this age?"

"It was only a one-second indiscretion; and at least I am honest about it," added Keli, as he joined in self-deprecating laughter.

"I think your behaviour was your sub-conscious way of expressing your boredom and contempt. You were literally thumbing your nose at all those highfaluting directors, with their bureaucracy and interminable agenda papers."

"No. It was involuntary. I did not do it on purpose."

"That's exactly what I'm saying. You were acting subconsciously."

"So, I am not to blame then."

"Yes. I can just see that flake, perched on your agenda papers. A fragment of the profane, sitting pertly in the exalted company of Zunguzonga's best brains." Okolo continued to guffaw.

"I'm glad you are getting a big laugh out of the incident. But I can assure you it wasn't funny when it was happening."

Keli was permitting himself some silliness, in front of one of the few people on earth with whom he could let his guard down and be as silly as he wished. It was just like their childhood days all over again.

Suddenly, in the midst of all the laughter, Keli got up and gingerly closed the door. Okolo immediately knew that joking was over; there must be some serious business to discuss. Through long association and mutual trust, Okolo and Keli could read each other's actions, even if there were no words. Okolo was all ears, as he drew his chair closer to Keli.

"You know I sent you a message that I would be visiting home in about two weeks time," Keli began.

"Yes."

"I'm sure you're surprised to see me here so soon."

"Surprised, but very glad to see you again."

"Well, something important has developed."

There was silent anticipation from Okolo, while Keli tried to choose his words.

"It has to do with that my house in the city," Keli continued.

"Don't tell me the bank has written to you again."

"Not quite the bank this time. A few days ago, two men showed up at our house, unannounced. One of them claimed to be a lawyer. They said they came to inform me that I had lost my house. The other man standing beside the lawyer claimed to be the new owner of the house. And to add insult to injury, they produced documents purporting to confirm what they were saying."

"And did you confirm from the documents?"

"I did not even take a good look. I simply threw the documents back in their faces and banged the door."

"Very brave of you. So, have they come again since then?"

79

"No. But I begin to wonder what I myself should do next. Should I ignore them, sue them, or negotiate with them?"

"Do you think they will come again?"

"I hope not."

"Do you think they are genuine?"

"You mean the documents or the visitors?"

"Both."

"I don't know."

"This is really alarming," said Okolo. "I had thought you would play hide and seek with the bank for a few years, just like everybody else. But a precipitous turn of events like this was never in our calculations. That is, assuming that the visitors and their documents are genuine."

Okolo tried to maintain his composure. After more questions and answers, Okolo volunteered his advice.

"This threat certainly should not be ignored. At this stage there is really nothing to sue about, and I am not sure you even have money to embark on protracted legal action. I think that the best thing for now is to arrange a meeting with the impostors, to find out how true their claim is. Such a meeting should also clarify your true legal position and rights."

"So, you don't think I should ignore them?"

"No."

"Dada thinks the same way you do. I tend to agree with her, but it is reassuring to get some confirmation from you."

"Yes. I think you must try to see them very soon."

The sombre mood was just giving way to levity once again when they heard a knock on the door. It was Ojiso, Keli's father. He had come over from his small family house to chat with Keli. Apart from initial greetings and food exchanges, Keli had remained cloistered in his room since his arrival. Ojiso was seeking to socialize, and maybe discuss a few family matters. However, when he noticed that Okolo was visiting, he lingered only long enough to enquire after Okolo's relatives. He apologized for the intrusion, and then withdrew.

As Ojiso left, Keli walked with him for a few metres beyond the door, with the aim of conferring with him. He was anxious to find out what had prompted his father's coming. Ojiso rarely came to Keli's room except in very urgent or very serious circumstances. Custom dictated that if a father needed to speak to his son, he would send for the son, rather than go to the son. Keli and his father observed this pattern most of the time. In any case, Ojiso, being an elder, would not normally hold grave family discussions in the house belonging to someone as junior as Pali.

Ojiso wanted to avoid being alarmist, and tried to pass his visit off as merely routine. He only added, with some measure of truth, that he had noticed Keli's seclusion and dour mien since his arrival, and wanted to find out if everything was alright. Keli assured him that things were going well. Each person knew that the other had more to say, but the superficial assurances would do for now. That way, each one was assured of a good night's sleep before whatever lay behind the assurances would emerge. It was getting close to bedtime, at least for village folk; and with the visitor in the room yet to be discharged, both agreed not to bother meeting again that night. Keli promised to come over to the family house to meet with his father at the crack of dawn next morning. This was their accustomed time for discussing serious family matters. The solemnity of dawn, and the clarity of thought after a good night's rest, made this the preferred time for substantial deliberations.

Keli returned to his room to rejoin Okolo.

"I've always admired the way you and your father relate to each other," said Okolo, as Keli resumed his seat.

"Thank you."

"You know I lost my father when I was a child, so I've always envied those of you who still have fathers."

"Yes, our relationship is built on mutual respect. Remember that Pa Ojiso is barely literate and has not been exposed to much of the city or much of the world. But he is very knowledgeable in traditional values and traditional ways. He understands little of the external world, and trusts me to explain as much of it to him as he needs to know. He defers to me in modern matters, and I defer to him in traditional matters."

"That's nice. You make such a complimentary pair. And your relationship is ever so cordial."

"Well, it is not always so cordial. Have you forgotten how things were at the time I was looking for a wife."

"I remember it well. Your differences really came to the fore at that time."

"Yeah. He thought that all I needed in a spouse were respect for relatives, respect for tradition, and good housekeeping capabilities. Of course I wanted someone who was physically attractive, socially presentable, and sufficiently educated to be employable. I remember how several candidates that met Pa Ojiso's criteria were thrust forward by well-meaning relatives, only to be snubbed or ignored by me. I thank God that in the end, I found Dada, who managed to meet both modern and traditional criteria."

"Sure. She's proved to be quite a gem, thanks to her decent family background, and strict upbringing by her tradition-loving aunt. She encountered modernity when she went to the teachers' college, but was not intoxicated by it."

"Thank you," added Keli.

There was some silence, broken by Okolo after about a minute.

"Have you informed your father about the problem with your house in Magotown?" Okolo asked.

"Not really."

"Why so?"

"This house matter is another area where Pa Ojiso and I do not exactly see things the same way."

"How?"

"From the very beginning, his priority has always been for me to build a house in the village. But you remember the master plan that you and I developed shortly after I got married."

"I don't quite remember. Remind me."

"We agreed that the village house had a low priority. The strategy was to first focus on getting a house or houses in the city. Such houses would provide accommodation for me, and yield rental revenue, which would then finance a house in the village. The reverse is not possible, since a house in the village has no rental potential. Much as it satisfies traditional requirements, a house in the village is not a viable economic investment, and cannot yield revenue for building a house in the city. I recall that both Dada and you agreed to this plan."

"Yes. Yes. Now I remember."

"Good. The theoretical underpinnings of the plan were correct, but the execution is proving extremely problematic. Our house acquisition in the city has not gone smoothly, and far from being a revenue producer, it is proving to be a black hole into which our savings are being fruitlessly poured. My village house construction had never really taken off, and is becoming a social embarrassment to me and my family. What am I to do?"

Okolo did not attempt to answer the question.

"The most difficult part," continued Keli, "is having to face Pa Ojiso in these circumstances. He keeps saying that I need a house in Alaku as a declaration of my manhood. He believes that having discharged the marriage obligation, I should devote every penny of my savings towards erecting a house in the village. He repeatedly points out how several of my fellow civil servants, with lower seniority and lower salaries, have managed to put up respectable houses in the village. Even Pali who owns this house is often held up as a good example of such success."

"Maybe Pa Ojiso is right," interjected Okolo.

"I know he is not right in this case. What he does not know, and perhaps cannot know, are the devious ways and means by which junior officers are able to acquire their wealth. Pa strove so hard to inculcate high ethical values in us as we were growing up. It is strange that he is unknowingly undermining those values by putting pressure on me to perform at the level of others who have lower ethical standards."

"Maybe Pa Ojiso does not know any better."

"Maybe; but most of the villagers have a similar ambivalent attitude towards signs of affluence. Like everybody else, they bemoan the prevailing corruption in the country, in the government, and in official circles. They blame the rich and the powerful for fostering corruption. However, nobody seems to appreciate the key role that even common village folk play in fostering corruption. Their loathing of corruption is restricted to the corruption perpetrated by other people or other people's relatives. When it comes to their own relatives, their only concern is how much of the public cake the relatives can divert their way. They tolerate corruption among their own folk in well-placed positions, so long as the spoils of such corruption are lavished on them or on their village. I don't know whether it is their innate greed, or their degree of deprivation, that so predisposes these village folk to abet corruption."

"You're right," said Okolo. "I have seen such people here in Alaku. They feel no moral compunction in accepting lavish gifts from dubious sources. They unabashedly cavort at social events staged to boost the social standing of known corrupt individuals. Sometimes, it even goes beyond the toleration of corruption. I have seen relatives taunt honest officers for their timidity in not shovelling significant amounts of public resources in the direction of the kindred."

"It's really too bad," said Keli. "Consciously or unconsciously, relatives and village folk are significant contributors to the problem of official corruption. Their complicity is real and insidious. The hapless officer or civil servant is consigned to the task of feeding their endless appetites, or risking their chagrin if he dares to stop. Their pressure is often enough to tip the scales for an honest officer and point him in the direction of corruption."

It was now getting close to midnight, and Okolo indicated that it was well past his bedtime. He rose from his seat and offered his right hand to Keli. They held onto each other's hands in a lingering handshake, but nobody spoke. It was only after Keli had walked with Okolo for a few metres, as is customary, that traditional good-night greetings were exchanged. Okolo melted into the darkness, while Keli returned to the room, and soon to bed.

Chapter 8 – At the crack of dawn

Keli slept soundly, at least for the first part of the night. As night dragged on towards dawn, he woke up several times to check his watch to make sure he was punctual for his appointment with his father. By 5 a.m., he could already hear his father's stirrings in the family house. He got up, did some minor ablutions, and headed for the main house. Ojiso was already seated in the living room, partially pensive and partially trying to shake off the lingering remnants of the night's sleep. The air hung thick with the smell of burning kerosene, emanating from the hurricane lantern that stood on the corner table. As was usual, the lantern had burned on a low setting all night. Ojiso had not bothered to turn it up as he waited for Keli, so the room was bathed in the eerie glow of semi-darkness. All was silent, except for a ticking clock and the rhythmic snoring from an adjoining room.

Keli walked in and greeted his father in the formal, traditional way. This greeting consisted of a brief ritual of standing squarely in front of his father, and pounding his clenched his right fist into his open left palm three times, each time acclaiming his father with the word "Baa". With each pronouncement of the word, Ojiso nodded in approval. In less formal situations, only one fist pounding and saying of "Baa" would suffice. Greetings over, Keli took a seat close to Ojiso. Most of the household was still asleep, so the two would have to speak in hushed tones.

As Keli settled down to confer with his father, he fully expected to hear something about erecting a village house. Ojiso did not disappoint. But first, there were a few more pressing family matters to dispose of. The most pressing one had to do with Uju, Keli's younger sister. Uju had only been married a few years, but she was having serious marital problems. Basically, her husband had turned out to be a spouse abuser, subjecting Uju to physical torment at the slightest provocation. Uju had tolerated the situation to the limits of her endurance, and just last week, the dam broke. After the latest bout of beating, Uju literally ran away from their marital home. As expected in custom, she fled straight to her father's house. Having reported back to her parental home, she then decided to avoid the prying eyes of inquisitive villagers. Three days before Keli arrived in Alaku, she had gone on to stay with relatives in a neighbouring town. She was still there, evading detection by her husband's people, but awaiting instructions from her father and trusted relatives as to what her next move should be. As expected, her husband's people had already sent a delegation to her father's house to enquire after their wife, but emotions were still running too high for any meaningful deliberations to take place. The timing of Keli's visit home was fortuitous since it would help Ojiso and Uju to fashion an appropriate response to Uju's in-laws.

Uju's flight from her marital home had been surreptitious but sudden. She left without any of her belongings. More significantly, she fled without her two older children, who must now be missing their mother. Only the youngest child, not yet weaned, was by Uju's side when she ran away.

Keli and Ojiso deliberated at length on Uju's predicament.

"Uju seems to be having such a rough time in this her marriage," Ojiso said.

"So it seems."

"It was only seven weeks ago that they had a major crisis, before this one."

"I was not aware of that crisis."

"Oh, yes. I did not want to disturb you by contacting you in Magotown. Moreover, I think you were on an overseas trip then. I was just sitting here one Sunday afternoon when I got the message that Uju had run away, after fighting with her husband overnight."

"She ran to you here at home?"

"No. She went to the home of her husband's uncle. As you know, running to her husband's relatives is a sign of respect for them, and gives them a chance to try to sort things out. It is like she is lodging a complaint about her husband's misdeeds to her husband's relatives. Handling the matter within the husband's family protects the husband's honour in the eyes of outsiders. It shows that she is not seeking to abandon the marriage."

"So, what did the husband's uncle do?"

"Well, he and a couple of other elders waded into the matter. They admonished Uju's husband for his uncontrollable temper. They made him promise to desist from physically threatening Uju. So, after about three days, Uju returned to her husband."

"It now seems that the settlement did not work."

"Not from the look of things. Indeed, things look much worse now."

"How?"

"You notice that this time, Uju ran back to our home here; her paternal home. The situation is much more grave. She seems to have given up on the husband's relatives."

"And possibly on the husband as well."

"Possibly. But that would be a crying shame. All other aspects of the marriage seemed to be going well. If only this scourge of spousal abuse could be eliminated from it, things could be quite rosy. They have been blessed in many ways. Look at their three beautiful children."

"Yes. I really feel for those children. I am sure all this discord must be affecting them."

"Sure. But it would be even worse for them if Uju left the husband completely."

"I agree. If only for the sake of the children, we must continue to search for reconciliation. We must find a solution that permits Uju to go back with good assurances of safety, respect and happiness."

There was silence for about a minute, while each person presumably searched for ideas on how to handle Uju's marital problem.

"You know that in my job, I often go round giving lectures," Keli said, breaking the long silence.

"I know. You government people are full of talk-talk."

"Yes. But we talk sense most of the time."

"That's what you think, but I am not sure everybody agrees."

"Anyway, just two months ago, I was invited to give a talk at the college that Dada attended."

"The Teachers' College in Magotown?"

"Yes. And do you know what they asked me to speak about?"

"Tell me."

"Spousal abuse. That was the topic they gave me. Spousal abuse. I spoke to them at length about its evils, how it shows a lack of respect for the abused spouse, and how it is the number one cause of marriage breakdown in our society."

"Yes, it is such a common thing these days," Ojiso stated. "In my time, we used to respect our women a lot. I have had major disagreements with your mother, but I have never punched her. These days, you young men are so tense all the time. You work out your frustrations on your wives and use them as punching bags."

"Not all of us."

"Not all, but many. Too many. I don't know why your generation is so inclined to violence against your spouses. Of course, in earlier times, our society practiced polygamy. We could always marry another wife if the first one proved incompatible. Maybe that allowed us to be a bit more tolerant. We did not feel trapped with one person."

"You think people beat their wives because they feel trapped?" asked Keli.

"Not really; but who knows? That may be part of it. Since marrying another wife is out of the question for young people today, they feel trapped and frustrated. They become violent. The only alternative that they see is divorce. And that is a terrible alternative, because of what it does to the children. It tears them apart emotionally, socially, psychologically. It tears them apart in all ways short of physical."

"You are right," Keli agreed. "That's the way I see Uju's case too. If not for the hardship it would inflict on the three children, I would have long ago asked Uju to leave her marriage; to divorce that brute she has as a husband. But can you imagine those three children growing up without their father or without their mother?"

"That is why some people say that divorce is an answer that generates questions. It is a solution that creates problems. It provides an easy solution for the spouses, but generates problems for the children."

"It is like passing on the burden from the adults to the children," added Keli. "That is why I think that divorce should only be used as a last resort."

"But," asked Ojiso, "don't you think that the high rate of divorce now has to do with the frivolous and casual way that you young people choose your spouses these days? Young people of your generation often choose spouses casually, without seeking consensus among your relatives. All that matters is your own selfish judgment and satisfaction. So, if there is any turbulence in the marriage, there is nobody to mediate. The only thing left then is to rush into a divorce; again a selfish solution that shifts the load from the spouses to the children. Easy come, easy go; that's the way they see their spouse and marriage. A bit less selfishness in choosing the spouse may reduce the tensions in marriage; and a bit less selfishness in rushing for the divorce option may reduce the hardship on the children."

"Yes. I know that there are situations where divorce is definitely called for," said Keli, "but it is a solution that must be used sparingly. Many people use it hastily to lift the burden from their heads, not caring that the burden now lands on the children. It is like a selfish quick fix."

"Anyway, I am glad you're out there letting people know the evils of spousal abuse, and the importance of mutual respect in marriage."

"Yes. I talk about it often, formally and informally. Little did I know that I would be so directly challenged by this very scourge. Right in my own family."

"Strange. Anyway, it's good that you have some official expertise on the matter. That should help us find a solution for Uju."

"Well, you know how it is," replied Keli. "It is easier to see the speck in somebody else's eye, than the one in your own eye. Anyway, we'll try."

"So, what do you think?"

"My big concern is for those children that Uju left behind."

"Me, too."

"I think we should encourage Uju to return to her husband."

"Yes, those children must be missing her very badly."

"She must return there, but we will lay down some very strict conditions for the husband."

"Like what?"

"We will make it clear that if there is any further abuse, we will reconsider the entire relationship."

Both Keli and his father knew that such a threat to Uju's husband was not new. It had been laid down on several previous occasions when there was strain in the marriage. What would be new this time was a mechanism for enforcing the stipulation.

"All those relatives of Uju's husband must face up to their responsibilities," continued Keli. "They must keep him on the straight and narrow. If he fails, they fail, and we will not listen to them if they send another reconciliatory delegation to plead for him."

"Yes. They must realize that marriage in Alaku is a union between two families, not just two individuals. If the relatives do not play their supportive part, the marriage will not last."

"You will have to speak very sternly to Uju's in-laws."

"Don't worry. I know they are waiting for me to invite them for another reconciliatory meeting. I'll lay it all on the line then."

"Please do. I am getting tired of all this nonsense."

"Me too," added Ojiso.

"Now that we've decided what to do about Uju," Ojiso continued, "let's move on to some developments around our family house here. More precisely, concerning your plot of land."

Keli adjusted himself on his seat, and braced himself for the usual barrage of arguments about why he needed to hurry up to put up a village house.

"Two days ago, I heard that somebody has cut a trail through your designated site. The information I got was vague, but I have not yet had time to go and take a look. I suggest that as soon as we are done talking, you and I should go and inspect the plot."

By this time in the discussion, Keli and his father were joined by Bedemu, who had awakened in an adjoining room. The boy alternated listlessly from parent to grandparent and back again. Although he could not comprehend what was being discussed, the three generations, gathered together in the hushed silence of dawn, presented a classic study in contrasts. There was Ojiso who had spent all his life in the village; then Keli whose early life was spent in the village while most of his latter life would be spent in the city; and finally, Bedemu who, apart from occasional visits to the village, was destined to spend all his life in the city. Destiny had laid different paths before each of them.

Now that they were discussing the matter of houses, Keli felt obliged to volunteer some information on his travails with respect to his house in Magotown. Partly because he knew that his father's priorities lay elsewhere, Keli was always sparing in what he told his father about his city house and the transactions surrounding it. Moreover, Ojiso's level of literacy made it superfluous to try to explain all the nuances of a modern-day real estate transaction. To Okolo, Keli could explicitly reveal everything and expect full compassion, full comprehension, and solid advice. To his father, he would only sketch the barest outlines and expect full compassion, limited comprehension, and grudging resignation.

On this occasion though, Keli felt that he must let his father know one of the possible outcomes of his present travails: that he might indeed lose the house in the city. This was the very house to which he had committed all his resources over the past several years; the house that had been his ready excuse for lack of progress on his village house. Keli began his narration rather circuitously.

"You know you have always tried to provide for me," he ventured.

"Yes?"

"That is exactly what I am trying to do for my children."

He raised his hand and gave a gentle pat on the head to Bedemu, who happened to be standing between his legs at the time.

"Yes, I want them to have a good future," Keli continued. "That is why I have been trying to secure that house that I bought in the city. I know you did not like the idea, but I did not do it for myself. I did it for them."

He patted Bedemu on the head again.

"Anyway, a slight problem has come up with respect to the house," Keli announced.

Ojiso straightened up in his chair.

"I have had a hard time keeping up with the payments on the house. In fact, I now owe a huge sum on it."

"How much?" Ojiso asked.

"I don't know, but it is big. However, the big problem now is that the bank that lent me the money to buy the house is trying to take the house away from me."

Keli ended his narration right there. He felt that there was no purpose served in bothering his father with the details of his troubles. He was particularly careful to avoid any mention of the visit to his house by Mr. Skoop and his lawyer.

When Keli's long pause indicated that no more details were forthcoming, his father chimed in.

"Strange things happen in these modern times, especially in cities like Magotown. Never in my sixty years of life have I seen a single person lose his house in the village to bankers, creditors or anybody else. Indeed, such a thing is alien to us and to village traditions. I am sure that such things can only happen in the city. This is why I have always favoured building a house here rather than in the city. Do you think if you had built the house here, any stranger would dare to come to Alaku to take it from you? It is just as if I knew. In any case, I really feel sorry that despite all your struggles, things are not working out well with that city house. I know you're doing your best and using your best judgment."

Ojiso's gloom was palpable, and Keli quickly stepped in to minimize the damage.

"Don't worry, Baa. I have everything under control."

"Well, I know these must be very difficult times for you and Dada. Try not to lose your composure."

Then leaning forward towards Keli and Bedemu, Ojiso added pointedly, "And never forget your family background and upbringing. The honour of our family stands above everything else. We may not be rich, but we guard our honesty and honour jealously. I know the city is full of temptations. But your shield against all temptations is the armour of honesty, which we have given you since you were a child. Stick to your high principles, and God will surely bless you."

The moral strength and anointing that Keli had come home to seek was being delivered in full. Okolo had delivered one aspect in the form of honest, concrete, specific advice; Ojiso, less knowledgeable about the details, was now delivering the other aspect in the form of moral and emotional fortification. Father and son might differ in their opinions, but at the deeper level of feelings and emotions, they were inseparable.

As the discussion went on, the light of dawn was becoming faintly visible, and other members of the household were beginning to stir. This household was made up of a curious amalgam of nuclear family members and live-in relatives from the extended family. Tradition dictated that on rising, each person had to seek out everyone who was older, to offer greetings. Each greeting, once offered, triggered a series of back and forth iterative greetings. By the time half a dozen members of the extended household were awake, Keli and Ojiso could no longer carry on their discussion without interruption. This or the other household member would emerge from the shadows and commence the greeting ritual, first with Ojiso, and then with Keli. The interruptions were becoming frequent and the father and son found it difficult to concentrate. Moreover, with so many ears now alert, the confidential atmosphere needed for serious family discussions had been lost. Neither discussant needed any reminding that it was time to wind up the meeting.

Chapter 9 – The dormant village plot

Keli and Ojiso left to inspect Keli's plot of land. Bedemu, curious as ever, trailed along. They took the winding path that ran eastward from the family house. A few metres down the path, they stopped to inspect three orange seedlings that Ojiso had transplanted a couple of days earlier. The seedlings were doing fine. Ojiso pointed out that in keeping with the pattern of intra-family exchanges in Alaku, he had nurtured the three orange saplings as his gift to Keli's three children. Bedemu quickly laid claim to the tallest of the seedlings, and promised to nurture it to maturity. The pace of this trio was leisurely, not even enough to break a sweat. As the winding path took them past a neighbour's house, they shouted out greetings to the awakening family. There was no response, but at least they had registered their presence, and signalled that they were passing through. They walked casually, stopping twice to let the trailing and distracted Bedemu catch up. In ten minutes, they were at the plot.

Keli had not been to the plot in many, many months and had trouble recognizing the site. It was virtually a piece of bush. Successive generations of weeds had germinated, flourished, flowered, and reseeded on the plot since Keli's last visit. There were climbers and shrubbery all over the place, with birds nesting on some of the denser clumps of shrubbery. Even the heaps of sand and gravel that had been deposited earlier could just barely be discerned in the thicket. What was not difficult to discern was a freshly-cut trail that ran diagonally across the dormant plot. Keli was alarmed, but his father did not seem to share his anxiety.

A cursory survey of the trail in Keli's plot showed that it led to a snare. The snare actually lay outside the plot, but the trail was the pathway through which the prospector walked to inspect his snare.

"I see. Somebody has been setting traps for bush meat around here," Ojiso said in a light casual manner. "I hope he succeeds."

"Whose trap do you think it is?" asked Keli anxiously.

"I don't know, but it must be one of our relatives."

"Relatives or not, they all know that you are the custodian of this plot while I am away in the city. Why did they not seek permission from you before going in here?"

"What permission?" asked Ojiso.

"Permission to enter."

"Why?"

"They must have known that it is our property."

"Yes, they know. Do you see them building a house on it?"

"But what about the trail. That is how encroachment usually starts."

"What encroachment?"

"So you don't think he means any harm?" asked Keli, his anger rising.

"This is nothing. When I got the report that something was going on here, I did not know how serious. Now I see it is just somebody looking for bush meat. I hope he catches what he is after."

"But do we know who it is?"

"Why do you want to know?"

"I want to know so I can keep an eye on him, and perhaps even give him a stern warning to keep away."

"They will just laugh at you. Everybody will laugh at you. In the village, a path like this is no trespass. You see, it is customary for villagers to traverse designated plots to try to make a living. They may be searching for wild game, laying snares for animals, collecting mushrooms, or similar things. When you own a piece of land here, it does not mean that others cannot use it. They can use it, so long as such use does not interfere with the intended use of the primary owner. As you know, the land belongs to all the people."

"Yes," added Keli. "I am told that is why they gave me this plot free of charge. In Magotown, I would have had to pay thousands of zungus for land like this. And over there, ownership is ownership. Rights to a plot of land are exclusive and absolute. No subsidiary uses by others are permitted, even if the primary owner of the plot has no immediate use for it. Even the mere act of walking through a designated plot is considered as trespassing. Large tracts of land lie idle, fenced off by their rich purchasers. The most that ordinary city folk can do is cast envious glances. Trespass, even in the form of physically walking through, is strictly prohibited and severely punished."

"That's a very greedy system you people have. Here, you take what you need, and leave the rest for others. Don't worry, whoever cut the path through your plot meant no harm."

"I still would like to know who did it."

"If you really want to know, I can find out. But truly, it doesn't matter."

Standing in front of his plot, Keli could not help but feel the sheer weight of the construction burden that lay before him, a burden whose gravity was being multiplied by the unsavoury developments in Magotown. For now, at any rate, he was relieved that the integrity of his rights to the plot had not been infringed. No substantive trespassing had occurred on the plot.

On their way back to the house, the trio stopped over at the house of Obi, the neighbour whom they had hailed on their way to the plot. Obi had awakened, and was busy hunched over a slab of stone, sharpening his machete in preparation for a brief foray into the bush. He offered two seats to the adult pair, but only Ojiso sat down. Keli was obliged to remain standing, in deference to the fact that Obi, his senior in age, was not seated. Bedemu found his usual place, nestled between Ojiso's bent knees. His entire attention was devoted to exploring a moth that he had picked up along the way, while the three adults chatted briefly in the warming rays of the rising sun.

"You both are up early," said Obi, grinning.

"Sure," replied Ojiso.

"And was it not you that called out to me about half an hour ago? I was just rounding off my sleep then."

"I know you normally wake up early to get some farm work done before the hot sun shows up," replied Ojiso.

"Yes, today is an exception. I went to bed very late. That's why I have let the sun get up before me today." Obi grinned again, revealing his full array of tobacco-stained front teeth.

Then turning to Keli, Obi added, "You city people never get up early like we do here."

"But then," replied Keli, "we never go to bed so early as you do here in the village. We often joke in the city that village people are like domestic fowl. They go to bed as soon as the sun goes down."

"You know we don't have electricity, which turns your night into day," Ojiso chimed in. "So, as soon as the sun goes to sleep, we follow its example and go to sleep, too. We do not have things like night clubs and television to distract us."

"How are things going generally in the city," asked Obi, testing the keenness of the machete blade on a banana leaf.

"Well, we are managing," replied Keli.

"What about Dada and the other children?"

"They're doing fine."

The conversation was going well enough, but Ojiso was keen to ferret out some specific information about Keli's plot. So, he changed the topic slightly.

"We have just been to Keli's plot over there."

"I am glad he is still maintaining an interest in it," said Obi. "I'm sure one of these days, he will surprise us with a mansion on that plot of land."

"Yes. We went to take a look. It is so very bushy," said Keli.

"Yeah. Bushes grow very fast during the rainy season like this," volunteered Obi.

"I noticed that somebody has been setting snares near that plot," said Ojiso.

"You mean the snares for bush meat?" asked Obi.

"Yes."

"I saw my son cutting a path through there two days ago. You know he is a very keen hunter and prospector for wild game. I try to encourage him to do his own thing, especially now that he is a teenager, almost a man. I hope he did not damage anything on the plot."

"No. Not at all. And we wish him luck," replied Ojiso.

"He never catches anything big. But I think the exercise and practice are good for him."

"So where is he now?" asked Ojiso.

"He has not yet come home from last night's hunt. But he should be here shortly."

"Greet him for me when he returns. Tell him that we wish him the best of luck."

The information needed had been gleaned. Keli's anxiety was soothed. The trail, and the snare to which it led, represented no attempt to take over the plot. This was normal practice. No harm was intended, no feelings were hurt, and no apologies were needed.

Early morning was no time for idle chit-chat in the village. It was a period to mobilize for the day's farm work or other chores. So, Keli and Ojiso were soon on their feet and bidding goodbye to their neighbour. As they were leaving, Obi reminded them of the traditional *Ozizi* festival, which would take place at the village square later that day. Bedemu, who had not heard about the traditional festival before, jumped up in excitement as he coaxed his grandfather into promising to take him to the festival. Bedemu did not have to try too hard. There and then, he extracted a promise from Ojiso that he would take him there.

Ozizi was the second most sacred festival among the practitioners of the traditional religion in Alaku. It involved animal sacrifice, propitiation of the spirits of the ancestors, and, in the eyes of some people, plain unadulterated idolatry. Ojiso was a keen practitioner of this religion, as had been his father before him. There was no clear-cut priesthood in the religion, but Ojiso was as close to one as you could get. He performed all the rituals, and was always present when others or the community performed theirs. He had an important role in the ceremonies coming up that afternoon, but Bedemu would tag along simply to enjoy the traditional dancing that accompanied the ceremonies. Ojiso was fully aware of the upcoming festival. He needed no reminding.

Keli needed reminding. More than that, he needed prodding. As a child, he attended the village primary school run by the Christian missionaries. He had encountered Christianity there, embraced it, and retained it as he worked his way through secondary school and university. He was now a staunch Christian, albeit a first generation one. Marriage to Dada, an equally staunch Christian, had given considerable reinforcement to his religious beliefs and practices. To him, much of what went on in the traditional religious practice was idolatry, pure and simple. As a Christian, he would have no part of it. And this included the *Ozizi* ceremonies.

Keli and his father parted after they returned from Obi's house. Ojiso and Bedemu went to the family house, while Keli repaired to his room at Pali's house.

Chapter 10 – Jungle jungle justice

Virtually everybody in Keli's family had their minds set on the *Ozizi* festival. But not Keli. For one thing, he disdained the idolatry associated with the festival. For another, he had seen the accompanying traditional dances many times before. They no longer interested him the way they once did. More than anything, his mind was too troubled for socializing on this particular visit. He was in no mood for the interminable number of village folk that he would have to meet again at the festival. What he needed most now was solace, time to be by himself and think deeply. Perhaps his imponderable problems might prove more manageable after such inward rumination.

Even before he left Magotown, Keli had decided that the best place he could be alone to think was Jekosu, the impenetrable and rarely visited forest that was part of Alaku's communal lands. Jekosu had been very jealously preserved by Alaku for centuries, and there were even folk tales about dragons and strange animals living there. To get there, Keli would need to travel about five kilometres up the Ako stream by canoe, and then walk about a kilometre through the bush. Jekosu was not frequented by villagers, partly because of the distance, and partly because of the denseness of the forest. Only the occasional hunter ventured there. Keli's plan was to somehow make his way to Jekosu, and spend an afternoon there in contemplative solitude. So, when Obi mentioned the festival, Keli immediately thought of the forest. With the collective attention of the village focused on the festival, this was a perfect day for him to be alone.

Okolo had a canoe that he used frequently for fishing. He would surely lend it to Keli just for the asking. Even though Keli had never paddled one, he felt he could manage. So, shortly after he left his father and son, and without waiting for breakfast, Keli headed across Alaku to Okolo's house.

Okolo was cleaning around the yard when Keli arrived.

"Achoo! How lucky I am to find you still at home," Keli said.

"Yes. We are all staying home today. You know today is the big day. *Ozizi.*"

"You are going?" enquired Keli

"Sure. I thought of mentioning it to you last night; but I know you usually do not like such things. In any case, we were so occupied with more weighty issues. Do you want to go?"

"Not really. I've come on a different matter."

"What?"

"I want to borrow your canoe."

"What for? You want to go fishing?"

"No. I want to go to Jekosu."

"You? Jekosu?"

"Yes. Jekosu."

"It is very far and very desolate you know. Especially today that everybody is going to the festival."

"That is why I have chosen to go today."

"You cannot be serious!"

"I am dead serious!"

"You will be dead alright. Who's going with you?"

"I'm going alone."

"Crazy! Absolutely crazy! You can't go there alone."

"I can manage."

"And how good are you at handling a canoe?"

"I have done it once or twice in my life."

"That's all?"

"That's all."

"Forget it, man."

"No. I think I can make it."

Okolo thought for a moment.

"You know what?" he said after the pause. "Let us wait till tomorrow and I will accompany you to Jekosu. If not for *Ozizi* today, we could have gone today."

"You're always so generous. But I am thinking of possibly going back to Magotown tomorrow. So, I either go today or not at all."

"That is really tough. I still don't think you should go alone. You need company. And you need somebody more familiar with the canoe."

Another period of silence ensued. Okolo, again, broke the silence.

"Okay. Let me ask Feli, my younger brother. He is inside the house. I know he doesn't much care for the festival. We'll see if he's available."

"Can he handle a canoe better that I can?"

"He takes it fishing frequently. So, he should know how to handle it."

"Feli-i-i-i!" Okolo called out to his brother.

The first call went unanswered.

"Feli-o-o-o!!" Okolo repeated after a brief pause and a deep breath.

The second call elicited a reverberating howl from within the family house. A short, boyish-looking man in his mid-twenties came running from the house. He greeted Keli, then walked straight up to Okolo.

"Have you finished inflating that bicycle tyre?" Okolo asked.

"Yes. I'm just trying to clean the bicycle now. I have finished washing; just wiping it dry."

Okolo wasted no time in getting to the point.

"Our brother here needs some help, Feli."

"What kind of help?"

"He needs somebody to escort him to Jekosu."

"Jekosu? When?" Feli was puzzled by the news.

"Have you ever been to Jekosu?" continued Okolo.

"Only two or three times in my life. The last time was about five years ago."

"Our brother wants to go there, and needs an escort."

"When?"

"Today."

"Today?"

"Today. I know you don't care much for the festival. Are you doing anything else today?"

"Well… let's see…."

The vagueness of the answer made it clear that even if Feli had other plans for the day, they were not terribly important. Okolo cut in quickly to complete the conscription.

"So, why don't you both leave in an hour or two?"

"Okay. I will get my fishing tackle together so that we can fish as we go along."

"Achoo! Thank you very much," said Keli. "I'll be here in about an hour. We can set off from the stream bank behind your house."

Keli returned to his room at Pali's. His breakfast had already come across from the main house. He ate skimpily, bubbling with excitement about his upcoming foray into the wilderness. With some bread and canned sardines that he had brought along from Magotown, he prepared some sandwiches to take along to the forest. He rummaged through his luggage for a novel that he had been reading for many weeks, but on which he was making very slow progress for lack of time. What better place to relax and dig into the novel than the lonely quietness of Jekosu, he thought.

Shortly after ten o'clock, Keli and his guide set out for Jekosu. Getting there was not easy. For the first quarter kilometre or so, there were dwelling houses on both banks of the stream. A teen-age girl in one of the stream-bank houses even recognized Feli and shouted out compliments. Houses gave way to stream-bank farms, again on both banks. The farms

112

grew fewer as Feli paddled on. By the time they had gone a kilometre, it was all dense forest on both sides. Feli laboriously paddled up the river for a couple of hours, explaining that neither he nor anybody else he knew had been to these parts recently. Eventually, the river narrowed, and the overhanging vegetation made further progress on the river impossible. So they moored the boat at the river bank.

Keli left his guide there and ventured inland on foot, partly out of curiosity, and partly in continuation of his search for isolation. About half a kilometre from the boat, he found a grassy patch under a huge tree, and decided that this was the ideal resting spot. He was as far from humanity as he had ever been, and was quite pleased that he just might be the first specimen of *Homo sapiens* that the plants and animals around him had ever made contact with. He settled down to have his lunch in this place which, from all indications, had not been visited by a human being in recent history. His plan was to have his lunch, read a little, think a lot, and perhaps take a peaceful nap before returning to the boat. He had found the most desolate spot on earth, and he knew it. He could hardly believe how well he had achieved his objective.

Keli was still unpacking his lunch when the air raid started. The first six-legged raider buzzed his ear. A mosquito. And it was not alone. Within minutes, he could see a couple of others swirling around his face. He waved them off casually and wished them good riddance. But no. They were back, and in even greater numbers. If they wanted a share of his lunch, he could well have obliged. But what they wanted was different. They wanted his blood; and he was not sure he had any to spare. In any case, there was no certainty that he could live with what the mosquitoes might give him in return. So, the battle lines were drawn. He swatted, flailed, and slapped frantically, but did not seem to be making any headway in repulsing or killing the enemy. With each swing on his part, they would retreat temporarily, then regroup and charge again in greater numbers. Occasionally, one of them would break through his defences, and perch peacefully on an exposed patch of his skin, sucking away merrily.

In ten minutes, Keli had succeeded in taking a total of two bites out of his lunch; much of his time and energy had been devoted to the battle at hand. After about fifteen minutes of his unsettled settling down, he decided to abort the excursion and flee from his attackers. He hastily packed up the remnants of his half-eaten lunch, and scampered back in the direction of the boat, totally disorganized, and barely managing to maintain a modicum of self respect. His persecutors followed. But he was too agile to give them a chance to perch. In any case, he was now too harried and flustered to take note of any ones that could have perched.

As he fled towards the boat, Keli found himself unable to comprehend what had just happened. It was clear that the mosquitoes did not come from the village with him. They had been in the forest all along, enjoying their merry lives without the benefit of his presence. This particular batch of mosquitoes certainly could not have ever encountered human beings since they were hatched. How was it, then, that these individuals, who had never tasted human blood before, were now behaving as if their lives could not go on without it? Their lives could have continued normally if Keli had not showed up; but now that he had showed up, their appetites had been aroused to the point where they felt that they could no longer do without him.

Feli was still setting up his fishing gear when Keli returned. He expressed surprise at Keli's sudden return. Since Keli offered no explanation for his sudden return, both men pretended that everything was normal. The guide reeled in his lines, and they turned the boat around for the return journey home. With his appetite for fishing still not satiated, Feli asked if he could stop at one of the deeper coves on the way home to try to catch some fish. Keli agreed. Apart from one or two other sentences, he said virtually nothing on their way home. His mind was still digesting the jungle justice that the mosquitoes had just meted out to him.

The cool of the evening had set in when the party reached their starting point. As they were mooring the boat, Okolo came running from the house. He had left the festival a bit early, and had been on the lookout for his best friend and his brother for the better part of half an hour. Okolo rushed at Keli, and both embraced and danced around momentarily. The ebullient welcome was just what Keli needed to lift him from his taciturn, contemplative gloom. Both friends walked towards the house, leaving Feli to finish the job of securing the boat.

Chairs were brought out and both friends sat down to enjoy the evening breeze on the veranda. Okolo was anxious to narrate to Keli the details of all that had happened at *Ozizi*. Keli, in turn, had at last found someone with whom he could share the curious adventure that had befallen him in the forest. Their usual joyful togetherness was once again holding sway.

It did not take long for Okolo to convince Keli to stay on for supper. The only cause for reluctance on Keli's part was the possibility that he might be departing for Magotown the following day. In that case, he needed to hurry home to say goodbye to his numerous relatives, and to pack his luggage. Still, his program was relatively flexible. So, once he accepted to stay on for supper, he knew that he had foreclosed the possibility of heading back to Magotown the following day. A one-day delay was not too much to sacrifice for a few more hours in Okolo's company.

While Okolo's relatives busied themselves with preparing supper, the two friends entwined each other in story-telling and pleasant conversation.

"Today's festival was the biggest I have ever seen," Okolo said. "Everybody was there."

"Everybody, except me."

"Except you."

"And how was the dancing?"

"Tremendous. There was this strange dancing group that had been invited from the village across the river."

"What kind of dance did they perform?"

"They had dancers on stilts who did all kinds of flips and acrobatics. They really stole the show."

"Yeah?"

"I spent most of my time watching them. I even saw Bedemu there also enjoying every minute of it."

"Yes. He must have been with my father. They went together."

"No. I think he was holding the hand of your father's sister. I presume your father must have been busy with the rituals inside the ceremonial hut. You know children are not allowed in there. Bedemu probably had more fun watching the dances outside anyway. So, how was your day?"

Keli did not immediately answer.

"Did you have a nice trip?" Okolo repeated.

"We spent most of the time fishing."

"But I thought you wanted to go and sit in the forest and enjoy your solitude."

"Yes. But that part of the trip did not last long."

"Why?"

"I was driven out of the forest."

"Driven out of the forest?"

"Yeah. I mean it."

"By whom? You must be joking."

"No. I am not joking."

"Who could have mustered the power and authority to drive you out of our forest, in our own hometown?"

"I was driven out by mosquitoes."

"Mosquitoes?"

"Mosquitoes."

"Shame on you. How could you have been driven out of the land of your heritage by mosquitoes."

"Well, it happened."

"How?"

"Let me explain. Immediately I settled down in the forest, this horde of mosquitoes descended on me, as if they had long been expecting me. Even though they must have been living contentedly before I arrived, it now appeared that they could no longer live without me."

"That always happens in the forest," added Okolo. "I've always wondered about it. It reminds me of my uncle Rudi. We are always reluctant to visit him. When we are not there, we hear that he is doing well, managing his own affairs, and thriving. But once you are there, he comes across as one whose life cannot go on without you. He falls to pieces once he sees us around. There are many people like that."

"Such people will stand up if there is no support," added Keli. "But once they see some support on the horizon, they lose the ability to stand on their own."

"Very well put."

"Yes. I am familiar with the phenomenon. At my ministry, we call it the 'dependency syndrome.'"

"You guys have a term for everything."

"These are people who can stand on their own, but would rather lean on you instead."

"It's annoying. They force you to support them, when your time and resources could be better spent on those who really cannot stand on their own."

"In our work, we find that this syndrome or disease does not operate only for individuals. You can also find it afflicting communities. This is what we see sometimes when I visit some communities with the minister. Some communities just want the government to provide everything for them. They seem unwilling to organize themselves to provide some amenities for themselves, or to mobilize for self-help. So when we visit, they give the impression that without the government, nothing could happen in their lives. Of course we know better. We provide what we can, knowing that they will somehow survive by providing the rest."

"So, that is how the government sees some poor communities like ours."

"Yes. But not all communities behave that way."

"Is Alaku one of the guilty communities?"

"I don't know. Don't ask me."

"It seems to me that the same principle can apply to countries as well."

"Sure," replied Keli.

"Could it be that the rich countries see some poor countries as having the dependency syndrome, as you call it? "

"Possibly."

"Where do you think our country fits in?"

"Honestly, I don't know how the rich countries perceive Zunguzonga. It is possible some of them see us as having a dependency syndrome. We try not to give them that impression. We do all we can to help ourselves. But who knows what they think?"

The conversation drifted on as dusk crept in. It continued through supper. Shortly after supper, Keli prepared to take his leave.

"Any new thoughts on our discussion of yesterday?" he enquired.

"I have thought some more about it; but I think where we left it is where it should be. Get in touch with those people and try to assess the extent of the danger that they pose."

They rose, and Okolo saw Keli off for a short distance. A long silent parting embrace was broken with Okolo's parting words.

"Let me know how things go."

The friends parted, and Keli wended his way home in the encroaching darkness, through the now-deserted streets of Alaku.

Immediately Keli got home, he went straight to his father's house. Bedemu had gone to bed. The excitement of the festival day had taken its toll. Everybody else in the household had gone to bed, except Ojiso who was keeping some sort of vigil waiting for Keli. Ojiso was equally fatigued from the day's exertions. He sprawled out on the easy chair in his small living room, half-asleep. The hurricane lantern on the windowsill, intentionally turned low, cast a yellowish ghostly glow on his weary frame. All was silent except for the timeless ticking of the pendulum clock hanging over the front door.

Ojiso was startled from his reverie when Keli walked in.

"Baa!" Keli greeted.

"How are you my son?"

"Fine."

"I was getting worried that you had stayed out so long. I even sent Bedemu to check if you had returned, just before he went to bed."

"Yes. I was at Okolo's. You know how it is when two of us get together."

"I know. So you had a good day then?"

"Good enough."

"What do you mean 'good enough'? How did you spend your day?"

"I spent the first part with Feli, Okolo's brother; then the evening with Okolo after he returned from the festival."

Keli did not want to volunteer the information that he had ventured to Jekosu, virtually alone. He knew Ojiso would chastise him for such folly.

"What about you, how was your day?" asked Keli, steering the conversation away from his exploits.

"It was a very long day, but everything went well."

"All the rituals and sacrifices went well?"

"No problem at all. I also ran into Dibie, the village medicine man. I made an appointment with him."

"Appointment? What for?"

Ojiso took a deep breath, and exhaled with a low audible groan.

"You see," he replied, lowering his voice and leaning forward towards Keli. "I have decided to seek help for some of the problems we discussed this morning. We cannot just sit and watch the problems grow. As you know, God helps those who help themselves. So we must help ourselves."

"So you want Dibie to help with Uju's problems."

"Yes. Uju's problems; but yours also. Especially yours. You live far way, and you need the protection of our ancestors even more than Uju does."

"Thanks for your concern. But of course you know it is against my religion to patronize people like Dibie."

"Never mind. You don't have to do anything. All that Dibie asked me to bring is the remnant of a piece of soap that you used for bathing, and that I already have. Don't worry, whether you believe or not, it is my duty to invoke the spirits of our ancestors to protect you in the city and help you with your problems."

"As you please, Baa."

"So, are you still leaving tomorrow? Ojiso asked after a pause. "I asked Bedemu but he was not sure".

"No. I decided to allow a little more time. We'll stay an extra day."

"Very good. That will give us some time to relax together tomorrow."

"And for me to hear some of those old time stories I love so much."

"Okay. I'll inform Bedemu when he wakes up, before he starts packing his things. We'll see you in the morning."

"Good night, Baa."

"Good night my son."

Ojiso stood and reached for the hurricane lamp. He turned it up a bit, and offered it to Keli.

"Here. Take this lamp. You don't want to step on any crawling things on the path."

"Thanks Baa. But I have a torch (flashlight) here. Okolo offered it to me."

"Okay. In any case, let me see you off a bit."

Ojiso walked with Keli for a few metres. Just as they were each other's first human contact for the day, Ojiso and Keli were each other's last human contact on this long eventful day. They parted and each one repaired hurriedly to bed.

Chapter 11 – Back to the urban jungle

During the three days that Keli was away in the village, Dada had been doing her bit to see how they could wriggle out of the problem relating to their house. She and Keli did not have many friends, and generally kept to themselves. She did not know where to turn. Then she remembered that Lego, her cousin, was a clerk at the Magistrates' Court. Lego was a not a lawyer, but had acquired considerable paralegal knowledge from many years at his job. Certainly in their circle of relatives, he would be the most knowledgeable about legal matters. So, Dada decided to visit him for advice and, as it were, consultations.

On the third day after Keli left for Alaku, Dada moved on her plan. She left home around noon. As is customary, she wanted to buy some minor gifts for Lego's family: fruit and pastries for the adults, sweets for the children. She decided to detour through the market on Wewak Street to make her purchases. As she approached Wewak Street, she could see people running from all directions towards the front of one of the electronics shops. A small crowd had gathered there, and there was excitement in the air.

Substantial damage had already been done before Dada arrived on the scene. The object of the stirring was a ragged-looking young man, just barely out of his teens. His head and chin were clean-shaven, except for a small prospective goatee that adorned his lower jaw. He wore a pair of oversized blue jeans held in place with a broad leather belt; but he was shirtless. There he was, crouching on all fours, in front of the shop from which he was accused of shoplifting. His mitigation plea was that for two years, he had been unsuccessful in finding a job. The plea was fully understandable to the crowd, most of whom were also unemployed. Through his heavy panting, the thief begged for mercy, indicating that the crackers and canned fish that he was caught stealing were to be his only hope for a meal that day. But mercy was in short supply. Blood flowed freely from his nose, evidence that some measure of instant justice had already been meted out to him. Glowering at him and hovering menacingly were three muscular men who apparently were instrumental in apprehending him.

It was some sort of stalemate at the time Dada became a spectator. Some beating had been done, but the object of the beating was not showing enough fight or resistance for his persecutors to feel justified in continuing to beat him. Yet it was clear that their appetite for further pummelling was far from satisfied. They were waiting for the faintest sign of resistance, so they could continue with their deed. But the victim was not obliging them. Apparently aware of their strategy, he was content to cower and remain still. He was also recovering from the devastation of the initial barrage of blows. Every few seconds, he would wipe blood from his nose. Tired of crouching, he slumped down into a coiled defensive posture. From his still, foetal position, his glassy eyes kept moving, shifting rapidly from one of his persecutors to the other, apprehensive that they might want to pounce again.

Dada watched the stalemate for about three minutes. Then the victim, having regained some confidence in his strength, suddenly made a dash for freedom. That was his undoing. His minders seemed to have been expecting his move. They immediately scurried after him, and with the help of men in the crowd, apprehended him before he could take five running steps. Now, no further provocation was needed for the tormentors to unleash their pent-up rage. The three men punched the accused freely and repeatedly until he finally slumped to the ground. Then, punching gave way to kicking, until the victim lay in a motionless heap on the ground, still breathing but apparently barely conscious. The kicking abated, but not completely. For the next five minutes or so, one or other of the persecutors would intermittently work up enough rage to deliver what he hoped would be a conclusive kick to the heap of flesh on the ground. The stalemate returned. The crowd was mesmerized and silent. The persecutors were silent. The victim was silent.

Suddenly, the gathered crowd was astir. A Toyota van swooped upon the scene. From the seat beside the driver, a burly, angry-looking man jumped out of the van and headed straight for the presumed thief, motionless on the ground. The new arrival delivered his own kick, as if to confirm that the object was kickable, or perhaps as some sort of *coup de grâce*. He then barked out a few orders. Without further ado, without finesse, and without mercy, the subdued victim was bundled unceremoniously into the back of the van. The three muscular men sat close to him, more in an attempt to prop him up, than out of any fear that he might recover enough to attempt an escape. The van, whose engine never stopped running all this time, had its doors slammed shut. In a moment, it sped off in the direction of the water tower. All that was left of it and its occupants was a voluminous trail of dust.

The crowd of on-lookers, Dada included, seemed to have been hypnotized by the spectacle. Throughout the episode, the crowd got involved only when the victim tried to run away; but once he had been re-apprehended, no bystander tried to intervene. Perhaps the perpetrators of the beating were part of a security company, perhaps part of a vigilante group. Two things were certain though: they were well organized, and they were led by that ferocious-looking commandant. Perhaps their reputation preceded them, and made it unwise for any member of the public to intervene. As for the victim, it is doubtful if he ever saw the courts of law, or even a regular police station. He had received some justice in the presence of the crowd, and probably had more of the same coming; more justice of the rough and ready kind.

For some three or four minutes after the van sped off, the crowd remained transfixed to the spot, as if the spectacle that attracted them in the first place was still there. Then slowly, in hushed contemplation, they began to drift off one by one. Dada herself was shocked by the incident that she had just beheld. All she could think about was how unjust the system could be to some people. The presumed shoplifter was already the victim of some injustice. She and Keli, in their own way, were also grappling with their own dose of injustice. It took her several minutes to gather herself together and re-focus on her mission.

Explaining the situation about their house to Lego was quite delicate for Dada. For one thing, she did not know if Keli would take offence that she was airing their dirty linen before relatives. And not just any relatives, but *her* relatives. By custom, the relatives of a man's wife were accorded the highest level of deference and respect. These relatives were constantly wooed with gifts and obligations, and were generally presented with nothing but the positive aspects of their sister's marital family. However, this façade also included shielding the woman's relatives from any adverse or untoward happenings in the man's family. So, how could Dada get the advice from her relative without compromising Keli's pride? She decided on the age-old strategy of presenting the issue, not as her own problem, but as a problem that one of her trusted friends had asked her to seek advice on.

The strategy worked, or at least it seemed to. The problem was presented to Lego as that of a friend. Lego accepted it as such, although given the emotion with which Dada presented the case, he might well have seen through the ploy and was simply pretending. Anyway, he listened attentively.

"I have this friend," Dada began. "She is one of my colleagues, a teacher in our school. She and her husband have a housing problem."

"Th...Th...Th...They're looking for a place to live?" asked Lego, revealing his incurable stammer.

"Not exactly. It is a problem with the house where they now live."

"Ok... Okay?"

" They bought the house with a loan from the bank. But then, they fell back on their mortgage repayments."

"How much do they n...nn...now owe?"

"I don't know exactly. But the bank has sent them letters threatening to foreclose on the property."

"How many letters."

"At least two, over the past eight months."

"And wha...wha...what did they do?"

"Nothing."

"Nothing?"

"Yes. And now, a man showed up at the house with a lawyer, claiming that the house now belongs to them. Is that possible?"

"How d...d..do you mean?"

"I hear that before they can repossess a house, they must advertise it, and then hold a public auction. And in any case, the owner of the house can redeem it at any stage by making payment," Dada said, parroting some of what Keli had told her.

"Theoretically, that is the p...prrr...process. You mean no adver...adver...advertisement or auction has been done?"

"I believe none. Do you think my friend and her husband should worry?"

The cousin paused a bit, while he deployed his limited legal knowledge to fashion some advice for Dada.

"Yes and no, is m...mmm...my answer. Sometimes they do these things in ss...secret."

"What things?"

"The advertisement and the auction. My ad... add...advice is for your friends not to take the th... threat of house repossession lightly. If I were in their position, I would have begun to p...ppp...panic and run around at the time that the final notices came from the bank. The b...bb...best course of action now is to seek a meeting with the lawyer and the p...ppp... purported new owner of the house. Your friend and her husband m...mmmm...may also try to meet with the bank officials. But I fear that if the lawyer and his client are ge...ge...ge...genuine, it may now be too late to discuss with the bank officials."

"What about going to court?"

"What for?"

"To challenge the repossession."

"It is a very, very long p...ppp...process. And very expensive too. I doubt if your friend can hire a b...bbb...better lawyer than the bank can. The odds would be stacked against her."

"So you don't advise going to court."

"At least not now. Let her find out the ge...ge... genuineness of the new claimant. Then she can take it from there."

"Thanks for your help."

"You are welcome."

There was a slight pause. Then Lego added, "In complicated problems like this, I always rely on God's intervention."

"How do you mean?" asked Dada.

"I mean that if I were your friend, I would commit everything to prayer. I wouldn't even rule out paying a visit to Pastor Emmanuel."

"Who is Pastor Emmanuel?"

"Pastor Emmanuel. Haven't you heard of P...P... Pastor Emmanuel, the miracle worker?"

"No. I haven't."

"Everybody has heard of Pastor Emmanuel. His prayer house is lo...lo...located opposite the police barracks at the southern end of town. It was my wife Maria that first m...made me aware of his practice. She had heard of him from some of her friends. Let me call her. I think she can tell you more."

Lego called out to Maria who was organizing some refreshments in the kitchen for the visitor.

"Maria. Please sit down," Lego entreated as Maria joined them in the living room. "Tell Dada about Pastor Emmanuel."

"Everybody knows about Pastor Emmanuel," said Maria. "Haven't you heard of Pastor Emmanuel?" she asked, turning to Dada.

"No," was the answer.

"Well, I got to know about him from one of my friends. She had a long-standing problem with miscarriages.

Then she started visiting the Pastor's prayer house. And do you know what?"

"What?"

"Within fifteen months, she gave birth to a bouncing baby boy. It was her first baby, and everybody knew it was a miracle."

"Hmm…"

"We ourselves have even gone to see the Pastor a couple of times. When Lego was having a serious problem at his workplace, we resorted to the prayer house and the pastor prayed over our problem. We know how things turned out. The Pastor's prayers really work!"

"See what I told you," added Lego. "I think your f…friend should try the pastor. God never fails."

"But what denomination is the pastor?" asked Dada.

"It doesn't matter," replied Maria. "Baptist, Anglican, Catholic, Methodist; you'll see all of them there. So long as you are a Christian, he will ask you to believe that his prayers will work for you. He himself says that he is a born-again Christian, with no specific denomination."

The rest of the visit was spent visiting with Lego's wife and children. Dada was not a frequent visitor to their house, so there was much to catch up on. She was very pleased that she had received advice not only on the main purpose of her visit, but also on possible spiritual solutions.

One day after Dada's visit to Lego, Keli and Bedemu headed back to Magotown. Keli felt that the main purpose of his visit to Alaku had been discharged, having consulted at length with both his father and Okolo. His thoughts once again began to turn towards Magotown and the unfinished business there. Before his present troubles, he had planned to spend nearly a week of his leave in the village. But his present travails could not permit such a luxury. He had to hurry back to stay on top of the situation. The extra day that he had allowed himself was spent quietly, bidding farewell to relatives, organizing his belongings, and organizing his thoughts.

As they embarked on the return journey, Bedemu was still bubbling with excitement at all that he had seen at the *Ozizi* festival. He spent the early part of the return journey narrating details of the events to Keli. As he wound up his tale, and noting Keli's apparent keenness at his narration, Bedemu added, "You should have come with us. It was very exciting."

"Sorry. I just couldn't go," Keli replied.

"I heard grandpa say that you consider *Ozizi* to be against your religion. Is that true?"

"Yes. It's a bit true."

"But it's not against grandpa's religion?"

"Yes. We have different religions."

"But the difference does not affect your relationship?"

"Not really. You see, each of us tolerates the differences, and we respect each other. He does not try to convert me, and I do not try to convert him. Occasionally, I even support him in his religion, and he supports me in mine. For example, you remember that last Easter, grandpa went to church with us. Similarly,

I sometimes provide him money for his traditional religious rites."

"So, do your two religions have anything in common?" inquired Bedemu.

"They have a lot in common. Let me give one example. Even though the two religions seem different, each of them emphasizes morality, honesty, and respect for human beings. Even before I attained school age, grandpa had already taught me these principles, which he, in turn, had derived from his traditional religion. Despite its animal sacrifice and ancestor worship, traditional religion was the source of the high moral standards that grandpa gave to me as a child."

"So what happened when you started going to school?"

"In school, I embraced Christianity. But do you know something? I found that Christianity taught the same moral principles that grandpa had taught me. There was no conflict, so I was able to build upon what I had learned at home. Maybe it is these similarities in our religions that removes religion as a factor in my relationship with grandpa."

"So, if I decide to take another religion when I grow up, you won't be opposed."

"Not at all. I think we have already laid the moral foundation for you. Any other religion that you embrace will only be building on it."

Bedemu spent the rest of the journey dozing in the back seat of the car.

Dada was not at home when Keli and Bedemu reached the house. Keli had a set of keys; so there was no problem gaining entry. One of Keli's first instincts was to check the left corner of the top drawer of the large dresser in the living room. That was where he and Dada usually left the bedroom key when they went out. That was also where Dada usually left a note if important messages arrived while Keli was away. The key was there. And sure enough, there were two letters that arrived in the mail, plus a folded note scribbled in Dada's cursive handwriting. Keli took a casual look at the two letters. Neither of them appeared particularly important; so he tossed them aside. He unfolded Dada's note. The message read: "The minister wants your advice on a speech he is preparing. Please contact him as soon as possible. This message was brought by his driver." Suddenly, Keli, the advice-seeking boy in the village had hurriedly transformed into the advice-giving man of authority in the city. But he was not in any particular hurry to get in touch with the minister. His personal problems would take precedence, especially now that he was on leave. He expected that the minister would understand.

When Dada returned home, she was bubbling with excitement as she welcomed her husband and her son from their trip. She soon sidled up to Keli to try to ascertain the results of his visit to Alaku, and possibly to compare notes with him.

"Welcome, KK."

"Thank you, dear."

"So, how are home people?" she enquired.

"Fine. Everybody is fine."

"Your parents and sisters all fine?"

"Yes."

"And what of Okolo?"

"He is doing quite well. His new position as deputy headmaster keeps him quite busy and quite excited."

"In addition to his hunting and farming."

"Yes."

"Did you discuss our house problem with him?"

"Sure. I discussed it at length with him."

"What does he think? What did he say?" asked Dada impatiently.

"Basically, he thinks the same way you do. He suggests that we should not ignore the visit by that fellow who is claiming that he now owns this house. He thinks that we should try to get in touch with them to determine what the truth of the matter is."

"And you think we should follow his advice?"

"Surely. Especially since it seems to be in line with your own original thinking."

Dada had also intended to share the results of her visit to Lego, even at the risk of incurring Keli's anger for taking their problems to her relatives. But it was now turning out that Okolo's advice was exactly the same as Lego's; and Keli was willing to follow Okolo's advice. So, rather than take the risk, Dada was content to leave well enough alone. She would not volunteer information on her discussion with Lego, or that she had even made the visit. Instead, she steered the conversation to other aspects of Keli's visit home.

"Bedemu tells me that they had the village festival while you were at home."

"Yes."

"How was it?"

"I didn't go. You know I don't usually like that kind of stuff."

"I know. So you stayed home?"

"No. On that day, I went on an adventure instead."

"Adventure. To where?"

"To Jekosu forest."

"Jekosu? I have never been there, and I am not sure any of my parents have ever been there. What gave you the idea?"

"I just wanted to be alone for a while and commune with nature."

"So, how was it?"

"Well, I experienced jungle justice. The mosquitoes felt that I was encroaching on their territory, and harassed me out of there in a hurry. Real jungle justice. Right there in the jungle. Who can blame them?"

"Poor you."

"Yes. I guess the jungle is their territory. So they are free to use jungle justice to drive me out."

There was a slight pause.

"There is jungle justice in the city too, you know," Dada continued.

"What do you mean?"

"I saw some of it yesterday on Wewak Street, when I went to buy some food. A shoplifter was receiving a heavy dose of jungle justice from some vigilante guards. They gave him a thorough beating, and then took him away, possibly for more. I almost cried at the injustice of it all."

"Yeah. The world is full of injustice. Look at what you and I are going through with respect to this house. Can anybody call that justice?"

"It is the same jungle justice that you and I are being subjected to."

"Yeah. We're seeing three tiers of jungle justice right before our eyes. You have the literal one in the jungle, the physical one on Wewak Street, and the equally painful figurative one with respect to our house. I tell you, whichever species of jungle justice it is, I see it as a very terrible thing."

"It is the worst kind of affliction."

"I don't mind jungle justice in the jungle. But right here in a supposedly civilized city? It really beats me."

"Me, too."

The conversation had inevitably drifted back to their present pressing problems. Their happy reunion was now tainted with exasperation, anxiety, and self-pity.

Chapter 12 – The mother tongue

As they prepared to go to bed that evening, each of the two younger children came forward to Keli and Dada and said, "Good night."

Bedemu was still in the bathroom, brushing his teeth. When he finished, it was his turn to bid his parents goodbye for the night. He went to Keli and Dada and greeted them, "Ojeoba!"

"What did you say?" asked Dada.

"I said 'Ojeoba!'"

Both parents, especially Dada, were quite surprised that Bedemu was greeting them in the traditional Alaku language, rather than in English as usual.

"Hey, my son," exclaimed Dada. "I see you have been practicing your Alaku language."

"Yes. Grandpa Ojiso taught me a lot of it when I went home," responded Bedemu. "He says he will teach me some more when I come home again."

"Very good," Keli chimed in. "I've always wanted to teach you Alaku, but I never seem to have the time. Your mother would have taught you, but she is not very fluent in it. As you know, she grew up in the city where people from all the various language groups have to adopt English as a common language."

"I like to speak Alaku," said Bedemu.

"Very good," affirmed Keli.

"And when I learn enough of Alaku language, I will teach the younger ones," concluded Bedemu, as he hugged each parent and went off to bed.

After Bedemu's departure, Keli returned to the discussion on language.

"Dada. You know, maybe Pa Ojiso is trying to tell us something. I am a bit ashamed that none of our children can speak Alaku fluently. The domestic language in our home here has been English. Now none of the children can speak our Alaku."

"Maybe it doesn't really matter," said Dada.

"It does matter. Their mates at school don't even believe them when they say they're from Alaku, since my children cannot back up the claim with the required language skills. If they cannot speak the language, where then lies their claim to being Alaku indigenes? Where have we failed?"

" No, we have not failed; at least judging from the fact that we've got plenty of company. Many other parents in Magotown and overseas are in the same awkward position. Their children have lost proficiency in the language of their ethnic group. Since they hardly ever get to use the native language, what use is it for them to acquire it anyway?"

"I'm surprised that you should say that."

"Yes. I say it because English is the country's official language; the *lingua franca*. That is what they speak at school. So, speaking it in the home as well actually helps the child to become a better student."

"Yeah. They become more proficient in English, but at what cultural cost? If the child speaks English at school, English on the street, and English in the home, where is he supposed to acquire proficiency in his mother tongue? Or you don't even think it is necessary to master the mother tongue?"

"Well; tell me."

"Indeed, learned people tell us that language is not just a means of communication; it also influences our thought processes, our world view, and our cultural perspective. Our mother tongue is therefore not just a means of communicating with others."

"What else is it?"

"It's a condensed package of our cultural being. It is our most significant identity symbol that proves our membership of our claimed ethnic group. Therefore, children who are denied their mother tongue are simultaneously denied an important aspect of the culture of their people. Left to me, the mother tongue should be declared an inalienable right of every child. It's indispensable for the child's normal cultural development."

"So, what else is the mother tongue good for?"

"Okay. Let's take a child like Bedemu for example. Here he is, growing up outside our native linguistic area. As such, he's denied most of the cultural activities and trappings of our people. Alaku festivals, rituals, rites of passage, traditional ceremonies, etc. are usually performed within the geographical confines of Alaku, and are not readily available for such a child to participate in or observe. But the situation is different when it comes to language. Language is, in a way, a portable aspect of culture. The child and the parents can indulge in it freely wherever they live, even outside the boundaries of their linguistic group. So, of all the facets of the native culture, the mother tongue is perhaps the most readily available to the child living outside their area of origin. If the child is now denied even this little aspect of culture, then he grows up in a cultural vacuum, since he is already denied most other aspects of his culture by sheer force of distance."

"It is like double jeopardy; either way he loses."

"Sure. I know you grew up in the city where fast foods are popular. So, I'll give you an analogy related to fast foods. While most aspects of the native culture are sedentary, the mother tongue is like a take-away slice of the indigenous culture. The family can take it wherever they go. Like the fast food take-away, it may not offer all the nutritional ingredients, but it can stave off cultural hunger and emaciation in the interim."

"You mean then that the Alaku language is a slice of Alaku culture that is readily available to the Alaku child growing up in Magotown."

"Yes. And not just Magotown. The language part of Alaku culture is available to the Alaku child growing up in London, Caracas, Sydney, Nairobi, or Manila. It is that portable. Even if we go and live overseas, Bedemu cannot enjoy the *Ozizi* or any other Alaku festival; but he can still indulge fully in the language part of Alaku culture."

"Actually, I thought that learning the Alaku language was only important for the Alaku indigene living in Alaku."

"Quite the contrary. The importance of the mother tongue for the child is in no way diminished by their living outside their native linguistic area. If anything, the mother tongue, in this case, takes on added significance. You see, the child living within her native linguistic area has some opportunity to practice and use her mother tongue on the street. The child living outside her linguistic area is denied such an opportunity. Her only meaningful contact with her mother tongue must be within the home. If the mother tongue is not available in the home, then it is not available at all. The need to offer the mother tongue in the home is therefore more imperative. Paradoxically, the pressure to install English as the domestic language is greater when living outside the linguistic area."

"If the home is the best place to offer the Alaku language to our children, then I am afraid we've failed woefully."

"Yes, I think we have."

"And I must accept a good part of the blame."

"Don't feel too bad. But I think we had an ideal situation to start with. We both hail from Alaku and could have easily insisted on communicating in Alaku in the home here. If that had happened even before Bedemu was born, he would have logically joined in speaking Alaku here at home. And once this critical mass of Alaku speakers was formed, subsequent children would simply have joined in."

"Yes, we missed the boat. I think the problem came from the fact that my mastery of Alaku language is poor. So, as a newly-married couple, we communicated only in English. When Bedemu came, he joined us in speaking English, and everybody else has followed suit. If only we had thought better of it in those early stages."

"It's still not too late for us. At least we both speak and identify with Alaku. Spare a thought for the situation where husband and wife come from different linguistic groups."

"Like Charlie at your office, and his wife Rita."

"Yeah. In such cases, you find that the path of least resistance is for them to adopt English as the domestic language in the home. The children are inevitably denied knowledge of both the indigenous language of their mother and that of their father."

"What a shame. I've seen a case though where the couple agreed to adopt the language of one of the spouses as the domestic language, which is then spoken by the children as well."

"It's the exception, but it does happen."

"It's a situation that requires a great deal of tolerance. In some cases, language conflicts can even wreck a marriage."

"Sometimes, the problem arises when the young couple engage a child-minder or nanny that is of a different ethnic and linguistic extraction."

"How?"

"The nanny invariably communicates with the child in the home in English; so that a beach-head is already established for the promotion of English as the domestic language. The family is now in a dilemma: either to operate in two different languages, or to take the easy way out and use English alone as the domestic language. Today's working executive parents, who spend so little time with the children, just cannot match the long hours that the nanny spends with the child each day. By default, they hand victory to the adoption of English in the home. The influence of the nanny can, in fact, subvert or subdue the initial efforts of the young couple to retain their mother tongue as the domestic language."

"Never under-estimate the influence of the nanny on the child."

"Never. Their influence can be more than that of the parents."

"This question of the indigenous language is really a problem in a lot of families these days," continued Dada. "But very few pay attention to the consequences."

"Very few. Many are raising children who are poorly grounded in their mother tongue. Such kids tend to grow up to be adults with dubious cultural identity. A lot of that is happening in the cities these days. This has progressively led to the production of a large number of cultural eunuchs who, having long lost contact with their home culture in deed, are now losing it in word as well. Worse still, such individuals tend to generate mostly their own kind. And the condition will perpetuate itself through the generations, until we find that a sizeable fraction of the ethnic group cannot even speak the language that identifies them."

"You think even Alaku people are guilty of this?"

"Yes. I see it happening even among Alaku people. There are many Alaku indigenes who cannot speak the Alaku language. They are unable to show the prima facie identity card to back up their claim to membership of the Alaku ethnic group. Their claim to membership of the ethnic group can only be nominal and spurious."

"I'm glad I can at least speak and understand the language."

"I've never heard of a Japanese person who cannot speak Japanese, or a German who cannot speak German. But we are starting to see Alaku people who cannot speak Alaku."

"What a shame. If an Englishman cannot speak English, where then lies his claim to being an English person?"

"In fact, what we're doing here, even in this house, is quite strange. Can you imagine a Spanish man, married to a Spanish woman of the same linguistic extraction, yet they and their children speak a totally different language at home? Yet, that is precisely the situation here in this house. We are both from Alaku, but have jettisoned the Alaku language in the home here, and have adopted a totally different language for use in the home. Shame on us."

"I'm sure we can do better in future; and we'll try to."

At the end of the discussion, Keli excused himself and went upstairs to arrange some papers. He was tired from the day's journey, and planned to go to bed early. Dada stayed on downstairs for another half hour, watching some programs on television. She, too, went upstairs shortly after 9 p.m., and then to bed.

Chapter 13 – Another three-way meeting

Exactly one week after the infamous visit by Mr. Skoop, Keli began to feel his way towards Mr. Skoop and his lawyer. Keli had met neither Mr. Skoop nor this lawyer prior to the visit. However, he had glimpsed the lawyer's name on the documents put forward during the visit. There were not more than a dozen lawyers in Magotown; so a brief reference to the directory put him on the right track. A few enquiries from neighbours and friends confirmed the identity, address and phone number of this lawyer. His name was Victor Tika, the principal, and indeed the only qualified lawyer, in the law firm of Tika and Associates. Mr. Tika was relatively new to the legal profession, having been called to the bar some four years earlier. He had spent the first three years as a junior partner in another law firm, and had only recently struck out on his own. His new firm was still on shaky legs; still struggling. But Mr. Tika was doing his best to make ends meet by accepting all kinds of briefs.

Keli telephoned the Tika chambers. A secretary answered. She indicated that Tika was away to court that day, but would be in the chambers the following day. She asked if Keli wanted to leave a message. Keli declined. She then asked if he could leave his name and phone number, so that Mr. Tika could call him back. Again, Keli declined, preferring to remain anonymous for now.

Keli telephoned again the following day. The secretary answered again, and connected him to the lawyer. Tika spoke.

"Hello."

"Hello. Is this Mr. Tika?"

"Yes. This is Victor Tika. What can I do for you, my friend?"

"I am the one whose house you visited last week."

"Last week?"

"Yes. You came with a fellow to tell me that my house had been forfeited."

"Oh! That visit."

"I am sure you remember it."

"I certainly do."

"Yes. I thought we should all meet together to try to iron things out."

"What things? There is nothing to iron out. When we were trying to reason with you, you thought we were joking. You even insulted us by throwing our papers all over the place."

"Let's see how we can resolve the matter," Keli entreated.

"Resolve what matter? From the legal standpoint, it is a very clear-cut case. As you know, I do the bidding of my client. The matter is resolved. The documents are all here. Unless you want to come and take a look."

"I thought we three could meet together."

"For what purpose?"

"To negotiate and sort things out."

"What things? It's a waste of time. If you want to have a look at the documents, I will oblige you. If you want my client to be present when you look, I will try to convince him to come. But I assure you that there will be no negotiation."

"OK. Let's fix a date for me and your client to be there."

"So, you want to come and take a look."

"Yes. With your client present."

"OK. Let's see. It turns out that my client will be coming in for some other matters on Thursday next week. Will that be suitable for you?"

"What time?"

"At two o'clock in the afternoon."

"Yes. Two o'clock on Thursday suits me."

"Thursday at two it is then. Do you know where my office is located?"

"I know the street number, so I can easily find it."

"Okay. We'll see you on Thursday then."

"Bye!"

Keli spent the next couple of days assembling as much documentation about the house as he could muster, as if his salvation lay in documentation. He collected and collated the warning letters from the bank; the purchase papers for the house; the loan application papers; his mortgage payment receipts; architect's drawings; the survey blueprints. Everything.

As part of his preparation for the meeting, Keli decided to photocopy all the documents he had assembled, just in case he needed to leave copies with the lawyer. The Wednesday before his appointment at Tika's, Keli saw fit to visit his own office at the ministry, partly to answer the minister's request for advice related to a speech. He discussed with the minister for nearly an hour, and was then excused to continue his leave. For another hour after he finished with the minister, Keli was busy at the photocopier adjacent to his office. Even though these were personal documents, he rationalized that there was some equity in using the office photocopier for them. If he could be summoned to work on the minister's speech during his personal leave time, then surely, nobody could begrudge him the use of the office machine for a few personal documents.

As Keli set out for Tika's chambers on Thursday afternoon, the original documents and their photocopies were all carefully folded into their respective files, and loaded in his work briefcase. He reckoned that he had armed himself adequately for this latest battle in the war to salvage his house.

Shortly before two o'clock on Thursday, Keli was at the Tika law office, as appointed. Mr. Skoop was already there, smoking and carrying on boisterously in the lawyer's waiting room. He was sitting, or rather slouching, with his corpulent mass distributed amorphously over a good part of a double settee. He remained in that position when Keli walked in. The two men greeted each other perfunctorily. Neither bothered with formal introductions, and Mr. Tika, who could have introduced them, was in the other room. Keli remained standing for about a minute, and in the absence of an offer of a seat, helped himself to a seat in the corner. This was the first substantive opportunity for Keli and Mr. Skoop to evaluate each other, and they made the best of it. Each paid a great deal of attention to the other's comportment and demeanour. Mr. Skoop soon got up, walked over to the lawyer in the next room, and returned momentarily to resume his slouch. Half a cigarette later, he hollered to Mr. Tika to hurry up and save everybody time.

Mr. Tika soon gathered up his papers from his desk, and ushered the pair into his meeting room. The trio got down to business. It was a business that was perceived quite differently by the two sides. As for Keli, he was there to find out what the purported transfer of house ownership was all about, and to show conclusively that there had been an error, or attempted fraud. As for Mr. Skoop, he was there to accept Keli's unconditional surrender. Indeed he was relishing the prospect of a double surrender: a surrender of Keli's pride, which had been in such prominence during their visit to the house; and, not insignificantly, a surrender of ownership of the contentious house.

Mr. Skoop did not need to speak. His lawyer did most of the talking. He explained the labyrinthine processes that had culminated in the transfer of ownership of the house to Mr. Skoop. He produced wads of documentation to show that all the proper procedures and steps had been followed. In conclusion, he swore on the honour of his legal certificate that all the transactions were genuine and straightforward. Then, Mr. Skoop chimed in with personal remarks intended to rub salt into Keli's wound.

"I hope it is all clear to you now," he said.

"I am sure he understands," echoed the lawyer. Mr. Skoop continued.

"We took the pains to come to your house to notify you. What response did we get? You were behaving like a peacock, full of yourself. You did not even have the humility to read the papers we brought. You threw them away. Now you waste our time by asking for this meeting."

Mr. Skoop paused long enough to catch his breath.

"It is people like you that are spoiling this country," he continued, pointing his right index finger at Keli. "You want to live in a big house that is beyond your means, when you know that you would have been better off renting from those who can afford it."

He paused briefly to observe the effect of his oration on Keli, who sat motionless. The onslaught continued.

"Long throat. That is what you are suffering from. Long throat and greed. You want this. You want that. You want everything, when you know that you cannot pay for it. In any case, did you not receive warnings from the bank? Why were you so careless as to ignore those warnings? Too proud to take notice. You have nobody but yourself to blame for your present predicament. Show him the documents and let us go," he concluded, turning to Tika.

Keli did his best to ignore the personal insults. He tried to concentrate on understanding his true legal position. Just as he had done at his doorway some two weeks earlier, he was orchestrating his last stand in the battle to save his house. He raised several points in succession, each one designed to prove that procedures had not been followed, and that the purported transfer of ownership was void. But the lawyer seemed to have an answer or document to counter each objection raised.

"The forfeiture and sale of the house were never advertised," asserted Keli, frantically looking for a legal manoeuvre out of his present morass.

"Sure it was," replied the lawyer, as he went on to produce a tiny clipping in fine print, culled from the classified pages of a local newspaper.

"Here it is," exclaimed Tika.

"Here is what?" asked Keli.

"The advertisement."

"You mean that was it?"

"Yes. It satisfies the law. As you know, I am a man of the law."

Even with his leave-time habit of poring over the papers, it would have taken Keli a lot of searching to find the tucked-away notice. That is, assuming that he was looking for it. Nobody who was reading the day's newspapers in a normal fashion could have noticed this obscure notice. The letter of the law and requirements had been met, but the spirit was certainly not there. All effort was made to ensure that Keli was kept unaware that the final *coup de grâce* on him was in progress.

"Alright," Keli battled on. "The law also states that a forfeited house could only be sold by public auction."

"Sure," replied Tika. "You seem to know the law quite well."

"But no auction was held in this case," asserted Keli.

"How do you know?" asked the lawyer.

"We live in the house, I and my family. There is always somebody there. If a public auction had been held, we would have known about it and even seen it. We never saw any auction being held."

The lawyer invited Mr. Skoop to respond.

"Sure, a public auction was held," asserted Mr. Skoop. "It took place the day before we visited your house to show you the papers. There were several witnesses. It was a crowded and hotly contested auction. I was the highest bidder. I was lucky to outbid them all. The lawyer has the papers if you want to see them."

What Mr. Skoop did not say was that there were only three people present at the farcical auction, an auction that Keli himself had unwittingly witnessed. The man with the bell was the registered auctioneer; the thin fellow in the grey native attire was the only witness; and Mr. Skoop's bid was the only bid, predetermined by all concerned in the conspiracy. These were the people that Keli and Dada saw from the balcony of their house on Bangumba Street that lazy vacation morning. They were not preachers. They were poachers. The only gospel they were preaching was one of avarice. It was a gospel that had nothing to do with Cupid, and everything to do with cupidity.

As if to seal the argument about the auction, the lawyer pulled out a sheaf of documents intended to confirm what Mr. Skoop was saying. It was all there in legally appropriate black and white, on large-sized paper, with all the stamps, seals and signatures in the designated places.

As Keli glanced at the pile of notarised documents laid out before him, he was struck by an entry at the top right hand corner of one of the pages. There, again in black and white, it indicated that the highest bid at the auction was twenty thousand zungus. That, incredibly, was what Mr. Skoop had paid for a house whose current market value was over ten times as much.

"Tell me, what was the highest bid at the auction?" Keli asked the lawyer, trying to confirm what he had just seen. "How much was paid for the house?"

"That's none of my business," replied Tika. "I get the documents from the auctioneer, and I go by the figures given to me."

"The price I paid is none of your business," concurred Mr. Skoop emphatically. "You have lost the house, and that is it."

A million questions raced through Keli's confused mind as Mr. Skoop and his lawyer gathered up the documentary ammunition that had been used to gun down the prey. Keli was slowly but belatedly coming to understand how the bank officials, Mr. Skoop, and other sinister operators had conspired to deprive him of his house. Keli's rout was complete.

On a note of monumental crassness, intended to mollify the devastated victim, Mr. Skoop added, "I know how you feel; but I will try to offer you a deal."

"What deal?" asked Keli.

"You don't know me well," continued Mr. Skoop, "but I am a very kind man. I'll give you a deal that will gladden your heart. I will give you two months within which to move out of that house. That will give you time to find another place. After that, you can stay on as my tenant for another six months if you wish. But eight months from now, you must pay up all remaining rent and vacate the house. I intend to move into that house by that time."

It is not clear whether Mr. Skoop expected an expression of gratitude from Keli, or an outburst of anger at the insensitivity of the offer. Neither reaction came from Keli, and outwardly at least, he simply ignored Mr. Skoop's insulting offer.

Chapter 14 – Seeking divine intervention

Keli managed to drag himself home after the bruising encounter with Mr. Skoop and his lawyer. As usual, Dada was waiting at home for the results of the meeting.

"It's just as we thought," Keli said, as soon as he had slipped into more comfortable house wear. "It's just what we thought."

"What, dear?"

"We're dealing with a bunch of crooks."

"You mean they are not genuine?"

"Well, some things about them are genuine. Therein lies our problem. The lawyer appears to be a qualified lawyer alright. And the documents they showed me all appeared to be genuine."

"And what did the documents say?"

"I was too flustered to study them carefully. But apparently they have colluded with the bank officials and sold our house in some sort of secret auction. Even the advertisement they were supposed to do about the event was done almost secretly. We just can't let such injustice go unchallenged."

"What shall we do?"

"We are going to fight them. If they can get a lawyer, I too, know where lawyers have their offices. We'll fight fire with fire. We've got justice and honesty on our side."

"But do we have the money?"

"Forget about money. There must be a way for people without money to obtain justice against crooks like these."

"Yes, but how?"

The question hung in the air unanswered, as both partners thought for a while.

"There's an idea I have been thinking about," continued Dada. "It may not solve our problem, but it will help us cope with it."

"What's your idea?"

"It's something I heard from one of my colleagues at school."

"What is it?

"Maybe we should seek divine intervention, some powerful spiritual help."

"How?"

"I heard of this pastor who works miracles with his prayers."

"Miracles?"

"Miracles. We certainly need one in our present troubles."

"So who is this miracle worker?"

"They call him Pastor Emmanuel. I hear he is very effective."

"Yes, I've heard such tales before. They all claim to see God."

"No. This one is different. Those who have tried him say that his prayers really work."

"So you are suggesting that we should go to his prayer house for help."

"Yes. It will do us good."

"Dada. I can't believe what you are saying. Have you forgotten our faith? We are Catholics, and our religion forbids us from patronizing shady religious groups, even if they promise miracles."

"This is not a shady group. I hear that he caters to all denominations. There is nothing wrong with Catholics going to his prayer house."

"Others can go, but we are not going."

"I don't see anything wrong with it."

"I see everything wrong with it. It will be a waste of our time and emotions."

"Don't dismiss it so quickly."

"Those people are worse than the devil. Don't let them tempt you."

"I am not tempted. I just think that they may be able to help us."

"Never mind that. They are too busy helping themselves."

"Aw…"

"We're not going. And that's final." Keli's voice was now rising, giving vent to pent-up frustration. Dada sensed the passion, and backed off from the argument momentarily. After a few moments, she continued.

"So, you don't want us to go to Pastor Emmanuel?"

"No. I don't want to go to Pastor Emmanuel or any other such pastor. The only spiritual help I need is already available within our church."

"Okay. Suppose we leave you out of it. Suppose I go alone to Pastor Emmanuel, will you still be opposed?"

"I will still consider it unnecessary and a waste of your time."

"But I don't mind investing the time."

"I can see you are hell-bent on going. In that case, I can't stop you."

"Oh, thank you. Thank you."

"I wish I was as convinced as you are. I commend your desire to leave no stone unturned. I suppose unusual things drive people to do unusual things. Go ahead, if you feel driven to that line of action."

"It's the least I can do."

Three days later, Dada took advantage of her lunch-time break from school to pay a surreptitious visit to Maria at her home. Neither Keli nor Lego was supposed to know of this visit. Lego was away at work, which was just the way Dada wanted it. Maria, a stay-at home seamstress, was busy sewing in the living room.

"Come in," she said when she heard Dada's knock on the door "Come in. Welcome."

"Thank you."

"Welcome. I did not expect to see you again so soon."

"Me, too. I just took a little break from work."

"Welcome. Let me get you a drink from the fridge."

"Don't worry. I've just had lunch."

"Welcome."

"Thanks. I just thought I should come and have a little woman to woman talk with you."

"I always like that kind of talk," said Maria, folding up the dress that she had been working on. "I'm all ears."

"You remember the other day I came here for discussions with Lego."

"Yes?"

"You told me about this pastor, Pastor Emmanuel."

"Yes? You want to know more about him?"

"Yes. I was looking for help for my friend who has some problems. But since you told me about the pastor, I was wondering whether I and my family might take our problems to him as well."

"I don't blame you. As I told you, Lego and I have already been to him; and the results were good."

"How does one make their way to the pastor."

"You really want to go?"

"Yes."

"You and Keli?"

"No. I alone. Keli is not interested."

"Hm…It is not advisable to go alone. Some people fall into a trance when they get there, and it is helpful if there is somebody to take care of them."

"I'll try to manage. Maybe I'll take Bedemu." They both laughed at the facetious suggestion.

"On a serious note, you need somebody to go with you."

"What about you?"

"Me?"

"Yes, you. Moreover, you've been there before and know your way around. Please."

"Alright. If you want me to come along, I will gladly escort you there. I'm sure Lego won't mind."

"This is a woman to woman matter. You don't even have to tell Lego, but that's up to you. I myself won't tell Keli. He's already told me he's not interested."

"You know how men are. They don't think the way we do."

"So, how do I get an appointment with the pastor?"

"I understand that most people usually make two visits. The first one is to get an appointment date. It is during that first visit that they tell you what to do or bring for the appointed day."

"Hmm…It sounds quite complicated."

"Not really."

"Can we make the appointment by phone?"

"There is no telephone in the prayer house. Apparently, the pastor does not believe in such gadgets. He and his staff say that they only believe in face-to-face communication with people."

"I guess we have no choice but to plan on two visits. When do you think we can go?"

"I am ready when you are."

"How long do you think each visit will last?"

"The first visit may not take more than a couple of hours; but you may need to budget half a day for the second visit."

"Okay. At least for the first visit, we can go after school. How about next Tuesday at about four in the evening?"

"That sounds good. Where do we meet?"

"Let's meet in front of the fabric store on Wewak Street. You remember the store where we both bought identical material last Christmas."

"Yes. I know the store. We'll meet there."

"Thanks for your help and understanding."

"As an in-law, you know there's nothing I won't do for you."

"Thank you."

Dada kept the visit brief and businesslike, hurrying back to her school before the break time was over.

On Tuesday morning, Dada let it be known to her family that she would be returning late from work on that day. Neither Keli nor the children asked why, and she did not volunteer a reason. Immediately after work, she took a taxi to Wewak Street for her rendezvous with Maria. As suspected, Maria was not waiting in front of the fabric shop, but was busy inside admiring the exotic fabrics on display.

"There you are," said Dada, as she spotted Maria in the corner.

"Yes. I came early so I could look at some of the new fabrics."

"Shall we go, or do you want to look around some more."

"No. Let's go."

Both women walked down a few metres to the taxi stand, and boarded a taxi for their destination.

Pastor Emmanuel's prayer house was tucked away on a side street, in the southern part of Magotown that had only recently been opened up. The main building was a large cavernous structure, painted all white on the exterior. This was the main hall for massed crusades and healing services. The inside walls of this main building were mostly blue with spots of white. Various religious murals adorned the walls at intervals. The main entrance to the building was a huge, ugly-looking iron double-panel door, with a cross inscribed on both panels. Near the far wall opposite the entrance was an elevated platform which served as some sort of altar. Behind the altar was a huge red cross painted on the far wall. The word "Hallelujah" was boldly inscribed beneath the cross. There were two adjoining buildings, symmetrically arranged - one on each side of the main building. The one on the left was elaborately painted and decorated, but the one on the right seemed to be only recently finished. It was not even painted but seemed to be fully in use all the same.

"We will have to go into the temple and wait there," muttered Maria, as they alighted from the taxi.

"You just lead and I'll follow," replied Dada.

The women entered the main building through the large door. The smell of burning candles and incense greeted them as they walked in. The place was very dimly lit, with most of the light coming from one large candle near the entrance and an even larger one near the altar. Midway up the aisle, they picked out a place on the right side and sat down.

"It seems we are lucky," whispered Maria.

"How?" asked Dada.

"I can see there are very few people," replied Maria, looking around to assess the situation. "That means we may not have to wait long."

Dada nodded, and cast her own surveying glance around the place. The other people in the temple consisted of an elderly couple seated near the entrance, a woman kneeling in passionate audible prayer in the front row, a party of three women and a young boy, and a sprinkling of four or five individuals each seated separately and silently. Dada and Maria also sat in silent vigil. Occasionally, the silence would be broken by a new arrival entering from the rear; but nobody was leaving.

After a silent wait of about forty-five minutes, a small bell rang and a side door opened. Out came a short bearded man, clad in a flowing white robe.

"That must be the Pastor," whispered Dada in excitement.

"I don't think so," said Maria, "but I think things are starting to happen."

The bearded man walked slowly to the base of the altar, rang his bell again, and said, "Those of you who have come for health problems, please follow me."

The elderly couple and the three women with the young boy got up and followed him out the side door and into the unpainted side building. Dada and Maria continued to wait.

Some fifteen minutes later, the bearded man repeated his ritual. This time he announced, "Those with problems related to your employment, please follow me." Only two people followed him out the side door. Five minutes later he was back. "Those with general family problems, please follow me."

Dada nudged Maria and they both got up. "Maybe I should wait for you here," said Maria on second thought. "They may be asking you intimate family questions."

"Never mind," said Dada. "Come along."

They both followed the bearded man. The woman praying frantically in the front row also followed, but nobody else. They passed through the side door, through the open compound, and into the barely-finished side building. The inside of this building looked very much like an office. There was a small waiting room, crowded with filing cabinets and all the usual office paraphernalia. The bearded man asked Maria and Dada to sit down in the waiting room, while he led the praying woman into an inner room. Some five minutes later, the woman emerged, and Dada was ushered into the inner room, with Maria following.

As soon as everybody was seated, the bearded man spoke.

"My name is Daniel," he said. "I am a disciple of Pastor Emmanuel." The women nodded.

"If you have been here before, I am sure you know the routine," continued Daniel. "For people like you with general family problems, the pastor would like you to do certain things before you come to see him. First, he would like you to fast for at least twenty-four hours before you come. You drink only water during that period. When coming, you bring along a large white handkerchief, a candle, a stick of incense, and a small bottle for holy water. We attend to people with your kind of problem every Wednesday and Saturday. Any questions?"

"I am the one with the problem," said Dada. "My sister here has come mainly to support me. Does she have to fast too, or bring any of the things you mentioned?"

"No. She does not have to fast or bring anything. She will do those when she comes for her own problems."

"And you said I can come on Wednesday or Saturday. Any specific time?"

"No specific time, but it is usually less crowded in the morning. The Pastor is a very busy man."

"And how much do we have to bring?" asked Dada.

"How much what?" replied Daniel.

"How much…er…how much money."

"Aw…Our ministry is not for money. We never charge for our services. We rely on the Lord. But we encourage people to donate generously to support the ministry. And some say that a generous donation clears the path for a favourable response to your prayers. Give generously and your problem will be easier to solve. As you know, God loves a cheerful giver. So, if possible, bring an appropriate donation when you are coming."

After a slight pause, Daniel said, "Well, if there are no other questions, please write your name in this register, so we know you have been registered."

Dada entered her name in the register.

"On the day you come back," said Daniel, "come straight to this room so we know you are here."

"We'll see you then when you return," concluded Daniel, flashing a wry smile and rising from his seat. "But don't wait too long."

"Okay," replied the women, and they were ushered out of the building. They walked the short distance to the main road and caught a taxi. Both women were silent for the first three or four minutes of their taxi ride, each one digesting the extraordinary experience they had just been through. The taxi driver himself, out of courtesy for their womanhood, was not inclined to open up conversation. It was Maria that broke the silence.

"So, when do you plan to go?"

"I am still thinking about it, but it will have to be a Saturday. I am at work on Wednesdays, and as you said, the second visit usually takes several hours."

"You're right."

"What about you. Do you think a Saturday will suit you?"

"Well, we're already in it together. I'm sure we can find a suitable time."

"I need time to assemble all the things I will need. So, I don't think this Saturday will be good. How about the Saturday of next week? Are you doing anything in particular on that day?"

"I never plan that far ahead. It's only Lego who does things like that. I think Saturday of next week will be okay. Just send word to me early next week to confirm."

"Thank you very much, my dear sister."

The taxi first dropped off Maria, and then drove to Bangumba Street to drop off Dada.

Dada did not brief Keli about her initial visit to the prayer house. However, she felt obliged to somehow let Keli know that she was implementing her plan. So, on the Thursday before the appointed Saturday, she let Keli know of her plans.

"You remember Pastor Emmanuel," she said shortly after dinner.

"Yes?"

"I will be going to see him on Saturday."

"The day after tomorrow?"

"Yes."

"I don't want to discourage you. But as I said, please count me out of it."

"Don't worry. I am not asking you to go."

"So, you re going alone then?"

"Not quite. Maria will be going with me. You remember Maria, Lego's wife."

"Maria knows the place?"

"Yes. And she has helped me find out what I need to take along."

"Like what?"

"Never mind. Just a few religious things."

"Like incense?"

"How do you know?"

"Walls have ears you know."

"No. Let's be serious. How did you know?"

"Yes, you think I don't have a nose. There's been a whiff of incense in our bedroom for the past couple of days, and I was wondering what it was all about. Now I know."

"Now you know."

"What else were you asked to do?"

"Nothing much. The only other thing is that I have to fast for a day before we go."

"So, you won't eat tomorrow."

"No. I won't."

"Too bad. Never mind. Bedemu and I will cook for the children and me."

At about ten o'clock in the morning on the appointed Saturday, Dada and Maria left for Pastor Emmanuel's prayer house. The required religious items were enclosed in a plastic bag, which in turn was ensconced in Dada's large handbag. As instructed, they went straight to the unfinished side building. There they met Daniel again. He made a note in his records that they were around, and then called out to another white-robed disciple to take them to the temple. As he was leading them to the temple, this disciple gave them instructions.

"Do you have the white cloth?" he asked.

"Yes. I have a white handkerchief," Dada replied.

"Very good. While you are waiting, open the white cloth and talk into it. Say all your problems into the white cloth, all the problems that you want us to pray for."

"Everything?"

"Everything. You off-load your problems onto the cloth. We will keep the cloth and the problems here, and pray over them for seven days. So we are working for you even when you are gone," he concluded with a chuckle.

As before, the temple was reeking with the odour of incense and burning candles. Unlike before, there were more than thirty people in the temple, and more seemed to be arriving by the minute. People were seated in the order of arrival, and the two women duly took their seat. Dada could see that the altar area, a picture of calm on the earlier visit, was now the site of frenetic activity. Several white-robed disciples were busy cleaning and organizing the altar area. Several large candles had already been lit, and a few unlit small ones were arrayed on a candle platform at the base of the altar. Occasionally, one of the disciples would turn from his maintenance duties, face the congregation, and intone one hymn or the other. The congregation would carry the tune for a while, and when it faltered or finished, dead silence would return to the temple, until another disciple saw fit to intone another hymn. In between the songs, Dada found time to whisper her problems and intentions into her white handkerchief. Time seemed to pass very slowly.

Some thirty minutes after Dada and Maria arrived, they saw the whole atmosphere change. A tall man in red flowing robes emerged from the decorated left side building. He was flanked on each side by a white-robed disciple. As he entered the temple, pandemonium swept through the gathered congregation. Most stood up in silence, but some were howling, and others were ululating and throwing themselves on the floor. Dada and Maria stood up reverently and silently, befitting the fact that they were now in the presence of the venerable Pastor Emmanuel. The pastor walked to the altar in calculated steps, and took a seat on a decorated chair facing the congregation.

"It seems that we're about to start," Dada whispered nervously to Maria.

"I think so. We'll see"

The pastor himself intoned a song, which was picked up by the congregation, lustily supported by the white-robed disciples. The song ended with the doxology, "Glory be to the father, and to the son...."

When the singing had died down, the pastor motioned to the congregation to sit down.

Dada and Maria were watching the proceedings very closely. The disciples began the process of leading members of the congregation, one set at a time, up to the altar for their all-important session with the pastor. Some people went alone, others as groups. It took over an hour before it was finally Dada's turn.

A barefoot disciple came to the pew and beckoned to Dada and Maria. They followed him to the foot of the altar. There they saw two large baskets: one containing monetary offerings, and one containing unopened packets of incense. On cue from the disciple, Dada deposited her monetary offering, contained in a small envelope, in the appropriate basket. She did the same with the incense, but was told to hold on to the handkerchief for now. The candle was taken from her, lit, and placed with the others on the candle platform. Then slowly, Dada was ushered up the steps to come face to face with the great pastor, with Maria staying back at the foot of the altar. The pastor beckoned that Dada should kneel down before him. He took the white handkerchief from her and placed it on a small table beside him. He then sprinkled a liberal dose of holy water over her head. Dada had her eyes closed, but she could hear incantations flow effusively from the pastor. He evoked virtually all the saints that are in heaven, maybe even some that are not. Each segment of prayer was brought to a close with the words, "...in the name of Jesus," his voice rising to a crescendo as he pronounced those words.

171

Finally, the praying abated. The pastor took the white handkerchief, and loosely ran it over Dada's face as if to wipe it. Then with a few more incantations, he dropped the handkerchief in a decorated basket on his left side. The basket already held numerous white handkerchiefs from the clients that preceded Dada. Before concluding, the pastor took out a small sacred amulet from his table and presented it to Dada.

The session over, Dada was led gingerly down the altar stairs by a disciple. Her footing was unsteady, possibly from the protracted kneeling, or possibly from the dizzying experience that she was going through. At the foot of the altar, Maria stepped forward to support Dada on one side while the disciple still held on to her on the other side. They led Dada delicately down the aisle, like post-operation nurses attending to a recuperating patient. Midway down the aisle and away from the waiting clients, they slowly eased Dada into one of the pews. The disciple let go of her and asked in a whisper, "Are you alright?"

"Fine," replied Dada.

"Okay. Where is the sacred amulet that the pastor gave you?"

"Here." Dada handed the amulet to him.

"Listen carefully," he said. "This holy object is meant to protect and help you with your problems. Have it around you all the time. Some wear it around the neck."

"Can she just keep it in her handbag?" asked Maria.

"That will also do. But one thing is important. Never expose it to the direct rays of the sun." Dada and Maria nodded repeatedly to show that they understood.

"Did you bring a container for holy water?" continued the disciple.

"Yes," answered Maria.

"As you leave the temple, there is a large drum of holy water near the door. You can fill your container there."

"How do we use the holy water?"

"Just sprinkle it around your house whenever you like." With those words, the attending disciple turned around abruptly and left. In a moment, he was attending to another client.

Maria sat down beside Dada. Their eyes met, and Dada smiled a broad, poignant, grateful smile. She was still speechless, and Maria was content to let her recover a bit more before any moves towards departure. They sat there for about ten minutes before Maria broke the silence.

"How are you feeling now?" she asked.

"Fine."

"Shall we think of going, or you want to rest some more?"

"I think we can go."

They both found their feet, and walked slowly towards the entrance of the temple. There, as instructed, they charged their container with holy water. They walked out the door, leaving the temple and its premises behind.

On their way home in the taxi, Dada was still evaluating her experience.

"Was this how the visit went when you and Lego came here?" she asked.

"Almost exactly. The only difference is that they did not give us holy water."

"What about the thing with the handkerchief?"

"It was the same."

"I thought the pastor was going to ask me questions about the nature of our problems."

"Well, it seems that's not how they operate. They say you put the problems in the handkerchief, give it to them, and they will pray over it."

"You think that's enough?"

"I don't know. But we just have to trust them. You must trust them for their prayers to work."

"If you say so," concluded Dada wistfully.

Keli, Bedemu and the other children were watching Saturday sports on television when Dada returned home. She just barely managed to drag herself through the door before throwing herself on the sofa. The fasting and the emotional drain of the temple experience had taken their toll. Keli turned down the television volume and went over to her.

"Are you alright, dear?" he asked.

"Yes. Just tired that's all."

"I know you are hungry too. We left some lunch for you. I'll warm it for you while you go upstairs and change."

By the time Dada came downstairs again, her lunch was ready. She ate ravenously, chasing down the food with large quantities of ginger ale, her favourite drink. Shortly after lunch, she went upstairs to try to sleep off her wearisome experience. Sleep was easy to come by, and she dozed for nearly two hours. By the time she woke up, the sports fans downstairs were still at it. Occasional howls of "Goal!!" from them confirmed to her that their favourite Saturday football program was playing.

Later that evening, Keli joined Dada upstairs. "How did your trip go?"

"Well. Very well."

"You were able to see the pastor."

"Yes."

"And what did he say?"

"He prayed over our problems and gave me some things."

'What things?"

"He gave me some holy water."

"Holy water? We can always get that from our priest after mass."

"He also gave us this holy amulet, which I will carry in my handbag."

"Hmm…Do you really believe in all that."

"Maria says that we have to believe for the pastor's prayers to work."

"Okay. I hope the prayers work."

There was momentary silence.

"Does it mean you will not be going to mass with us tomorrow morning?" Keli asked, breaking the silence.

"Why do you ask that? You know I never miss Sunday mass."

"Just checking. I thought maybe Pastor Emmanuel had convinced you to start attending his church."

"No. I am still where I am. I'm still a Catholic. I'm only supplementing that by trying different approaches to God. You never know whose prayers He may choose to answer."

"Okay. You try the approach that your spirit dictates. My own spirit tells me to stick to the faith that I know."

"It's all for the same purpose. Whichever one works out will be fine with us."

Chapter 15 – From party to parting

In the days following the meeting at the lawyer's office, Keli contemplated taking legal action to restore his rights to the house.

"I really feel violated," he said to Dada in one of his moments of despair. "I'm still thinking about hiring a lawyer to go after those crooks."

"They certainly deserve somebody to go after them," replied Dada, putting forward a line of reasoning that she had used repeatedly. "But where shall we get the money to waste on lawyers?"

"We should at least try. I'm just as much of a man as those crooks. At least, I can give them a run for their money."

"It has nothing to do with manhood. Remember, they are rich. What's more, a case like this could drag on for years. They won't run out of money for lawyers, but what about us? We'll be bankrupt in a few months. It's like throwing good money into a lost cause."

"So, you think our cause is lost?"

"I don't know how else to describe it. All we can hope for is a miracle."

In a final desperate search for a lifeline to save his house, Keli went in search of Juwe. Yes, Juwe Galena, the bank official's cousin who had a virtual monopoly on access to the loan machinery at the bank. In the decade or so since Keli got the bank loan, his contacts with Juwe had grown progressively attenuated. They had found each other mutually useful for a while, but had allowed the relationship to decay when there was no further use for it. Now Keli wanted to resuscitate the connection. As usual, the meeting place was Juwe's workshop, which, despite all the fluctuations in the economy, had managed to remain operational. Juwe, too, was still engaged in his own trademark brand of the real estate business, and probably needed to keep the workshop going anyway, if only to provide a convincing front.

Keli drove to the "Junk to Juwel" workshop to find Juwe. The businessman was sitting in the elaborate reception room of his now-expanded and refurbished workshop. A manual calculator and piles of documents on the table indicated that he was tallying some financial figures, possibly related to the workshop, but quite probably not. A half-drained bottle of beer sat beside the documents. There was no glass, but the furious effervescence in the bottle made it clear that it had just been opened. Juwe was in the middle of yet another sip when Keli walked in. He put the bottle down, and stood up to welcome Keli. They embraced like old friends. Neither of them seemed to mind that they had not kept up contact with each other.

"So, how are things with you?" asked Juwe.

"Fine. Very fine," replied Keli, in a spate of polite falsehood.

"I haven't seen you in ages."

"Same here."

"I was beginning to wonder if you had been transferred to another station. We know you civil servants are always being moved around."

"No. I've been here all along. Just lying low, that's all."

"So, what can I do for you this time? You've come to work on your car; or maybe for some more real estate?"

"I don't really know. But I think we'll talk real estate."

"Great. I knew you would acquire the appetite for more houses. The way you started is the way most of my customers begin. But once they get the hang of it, they keep coming back for more."

"Amazing."

"Are you now ready to buy another house? I'm sure you must be enjoying the small one we helped you with the other time."

Apparently, Juwe had not heard of Keli's troubles with his house. Juwe's specialty was helping people with loans and getting them into the mortgage stream. What happened at the other end of the stream was not of much concern to him. There were other specialists, like Mr. Skoop, that took care of the other end of the business.

"Yes. That house that you helped me buy," replied Keli. "It is proving to be a problem, you know."

"How? Houses I sell are very carefully selected, and never lead to problems. The title is genuine. In fact, I don't deal with houses whose titles are questionable."

"The problem is not with the title."

"What then?"

"It is with my repayment. I thought Gordon at the bank might have told you."

"No. He did not tell me. As a rule, Gordon and I never discuss old business. I am all the time looking for new material. That takes up all our time when we meet."

"Anyway. The bank says I am owing too much, and has been threatening to take the house away from me."

"Is that?"

"Yeah. I have been struggling with the problem for a couple of years now. Do you think you can help me?"

"How?"

"To sort out the mess with the mortgage."

"I know you're a good man. Unfortunately, I don't deal with default cases or forfeiture cases."

"I didn't know that. But I am sure you can help me somehow."

"How?"

"You can at least help me contact your cousin who assisted us with the loan."

"As I said, I only discuss new business with Gordon. What I can do for you is this. I will find an opportunity to get both of you together. Then, you can present your case to him yourself."

"How soon?"

"I don't know. Come back in about three days time. I will go to his office to find out when he may be willing to see you."

"Okay. I will come back in three days."

A bottle of beer was offered, but Keli declined. The conversation wound up and Keli took his leave.

Three days later, Keli was back at Juwe's workshop.

"Were you able to visit Gordon, as promised?" Keli asked.

"Sort of," was the answer.

"Sort of, how?"

"I was at his office, but the whole place was upside down. He was relocating to another office, and the new occupant was just moving in. I could not really discuss anything with him. In fact, I could just barely say hello to him in all the confusion. I think it all has to do with his recent promotion."

"Promotion?"

"Yes. He was recently promoted at the office. I forgot to tell you earlier. In fact, he is holding a party for it next week. I intend to go. Maybe I can find out his schedule for you when I meet him at the party."

"Would it be too much if I went along with you?"

"To where?"

"To the party. Or is it for relatives only?"

"Not really. But Gordon forbids us to bring clients to his house."

"I'll try not to talk business; only to find out when he will be available."

"They sent me an invitation card for the party. But there will be other well-wishers there. If you promise not to talk business there, I am sure Gordon won't mind. I don't see why you cannot come along."

"Thanks."

"Gordon will probably be very busy at the party. It will not be possible or proper to discuss your problem with him there. But, you can get reacquainted, and perhaps make an appointment to meet."

"Thanks again. What day is the party?"

"Saturday next week, starting about five o'clock in the evening. I'll come by your house to collect you."

"Any special attire?"

"Nothing special. You can wear whatever pleases you."

"Thanks. We'll see you."

Juwe was at Keli's place just before six o'clock on Saturday. For what had the makings of an all-night party, a bit of lateness could not be of much consequence. Keli and Dada had previously agreed that she would not go along. Despite entreaties from Juwe, they stuck to that decision. Only Keli joined Juwe in the car and they drove to Gordon Galena's home.

What passed for the banker's home was an elaborate palatial estate, sprawled out over two or three hectares. The entire spread, located on the outskirts of town, was screened from the main roadway by some 300 metres of bush. There was a gate near the main road, and another gate just in front of the main house. Each gate had a team of security guards. The main house was a two-storey mansion, about forty metres long, with manicured flowerpots hanging from the window ledges. Most of the half dozen or so bedrooms were upstairs, along with a private family living room. The ground floor consisted of a large, ornate sitting room for receiving visitors, a small library, and a kitchen. Behind the main house lay a large quadrangle, demarcated by pavilion-like buildings on both sides. At the southernmost flank of the property, and running parallel to the main house, was another two-storey building, much more modest than the main house, but substantial enough to house several of Gordon's household staff and relatives. Keli could not believe that such an aristocratic setting existed just a short distance from the squalor of the city. Nor could he digest the fact that all this belonged to a bank official whose nominal salary was not higher than that of a Deputy Director in the civil service. While Keli was struggling to retain his modest house, Gordon was wallowing in the opulence of his extensive real estate holdings.

Seats for the party had been arranged on the veranda and the forefront of one of the pavilions. The opposite pavilion was to serve as the high table, reserved exclusively for the host and his immediate family. Inevitably, there was a place for the master of ceremony on one side of the high table. The riggings of a microphone marked the place.

When Keli and Juwe arrived, there were already at least thirty guests standing around, and the number kept growing by the minute. These early general invitees were seated in the veranda of the pavilion, with a few of them spilling over onto the grass on the quadrangle. As Juwe and Keli passed through the main house on their way to the pavilion, Juwe stopped two or three times to greet relatives who recognized him. He had desired to greet Gordon as well, but Gordon was not around. He and the Master of Ceremony (MC) for the party had driven out to collect some women who hailed from his village. These were members of the Magotown branch of the Women Association of Gordon's home village. These women were almost literally the life of the party. Some of them were already on the premises, doing the cooking for the party. The group that Gordon had gone to fetch would do the serving. They would generally act as hostesses to ensure the success of the party thrown by their brother who had made good. Yet another batch of the Women Association members had, for weeks, been rehearsing traditional dances that they would use to liven up this party.

Keli did not particularly care to mingle or be recognized. He was out of his element. This was not his kind of crowd, and in any case, his invitation to the party was only second hand, through Juwe. So, when they finally reached the party area behind the main house, Keli nudged Juwe into picking a seat in an obscure corner of the pavilion. Like everybody else, they sat down and waited for the party to get going. They chatted to pass the time.

"Did they say that Gordon went out with the MC?" asked Keli.

"Yes. They went to bring our women. The women from our village."

"Is the MC from your village as well?"

"I don't know, but I doubt it. It's not usual for a relative of the host to be the MC."

"Who's the MC?"

"I am not really sure. It must be one of Gordon's bosom friends. On an occasion like this, you don't appoint just anybody to be MC. It has to be somebody close to the host. It's like the best man at a wedding."

The wait continued. After a few more minutes, a stream of about a dozen gaily clad women issued from the main house onto the quadrangle. They each carried one piece or the other of party paraphernalia: a covered tray of cooked rice; a maraca made of beaded calabash; a crate of soft drinks; a carton containing plates and cutlery; a medium-sized conga drum; a figure-eight drum; one more bouquet of flowers for the high table; a double gong. Also carried across the quadrangle was a sedate brown live goat, presumably intended as the gift from the Women Association to the celebrant. The party hostesses had arrived. Somebody at a neighbouring table whispered to Juwe that Gordon and the MC had returned from their mission. However, Gordon had proceeded to the very private quarters upstairs in the main house, and was not yet ready to make a public appearance. Juwe was keen to talk to Gordon before the party started, partly to register his presence, and partly to offer his assistance in running errands.

As soon as he heard that Gordon was around, Juwe got up to seek him out. He hesitated a bit while he and Keli contemplated whether Keli should come

185

along as well. Juwe was familiar with all corners of Gordon's home, and as a cousin, no part of the home was too private for him to roam, in his attempt to locate Gordon. The same could not be said for Keli. He was a stranger, and would not normally go beyond the more public areas in the estate. So, it was decided that rather than cramp Juwe's style by accompanying him, Keli should stay behind, while Juwe went to seek out and converse with Gordon.

Juwe's absence seemed like an eternity to Keli. There he was, sitting alone at their table; in a sea of strangers; in an unfamiliar setting; on an uncertain mission connected with salvaging his house. On top of that, he was still doing his best not to be recognized or identified by anybody that might know him there. Relief was written all over his face when Juwe returned after about twenty minutes.

"So, how did it go?" Keli enquired expectantly.

"Well, it wasn't easy, but I was finally able to track down Gordon."

"How did your discussion go?"

"There is good news, and there is bad news."

"Tell me."

"The good news is that I was able to find him, and talk alone with him in the family living room upstairs. We talked for over five minutes without any disturbance."

"Were you able to bring up my matter?"

"Not quite. The other piece of news caused me to hold back on your matter."

"What?"

"He said that his new promotion means that he will be moving to another department in the bank. Who knows, he may even be moved to another city. In any case, he will no longer be in the loans section. So, even if there was anything he could have done to help you at this late stage, it is irrelevant now."

"Achoo! That's very sad indeed."

"Yes. But it is sad for me, too. Do you remember what my real estate business was built on? It was built on the people I was able to introduce to Gordon. If he is no longer in the loans department, then there is no business for me."

"Anyway," continued Juwe, consoling himself, "when one door closes, another one opens. There must be a way, even if I have to change to another line of business that will fit my brother's new position."

"Such is life," Keli added morosely.

Another ten minutes passed while everybody waited with heightened expectancy. Then, some stirrings behind the high table hinted that the party was about to come alive. The inevitable testing of the microphone gave way to the delivery of two bouquets of flowers to the high table. The high-table seats, which had hitherto been empty, were slowly filling up. But Gordon and his wife were yet to make their grand entrance. They were not scheduled to do so until everybody else was seated; then they would be ushered in by the MC.

Another round of ear-splitting microphone testing, and everything seemed ready to go. An announcer took hold of the microphone, and began to speak to the hushed crowd. "Ladies and gentlemen," he intoned, "I thank you for your patience. I would like to welcome you to this grand party organized in honour of a grand pillar of our society. My job is mainly to introduce the MC, who in turn will introduce the great man that we are honouring today. But I cannot resist the temptation to tell you about the greatness of our host, G-o-r-d-o-n G-a-l-e-n-a!" Loud, spontaneous applause erupted from the gathered throng. The speaker paused for a few seconds, and then continued.

"I have known Mr. Galena for many years. He is a perfect example of how you can rise from small beginnings to achieve greatness."

More applause, mixed in this time with banging on the drums and gongs, and shaking of the maracas.

"Gordon is not only known for his hard work, but he is one of the kindest people you will ever meet."

Still more applause followed, accompanied by sounds from the musical instruments, plus a few acclamatory whistles. The praise singing to the honour and glory of Gordon went on for another four minutes or so, with ever louder indication of approbation from the throng. If the announcer's brief was to warm up the faithful, he was succeeding immensely. Finally, he rounded off his oration.

"As you all know, we must have a competent person to pilot our affairs as this grand party progresses. Such a person is the Master of Ceremony. It is our great fortune this evening to have a very competent MC. He is a great friend of Gordon; a man about town in Magotown. Please give a hand for the great Hector Sikupah!!!"

The gathering erupted in huge and sustained applause. Some, like Keli and Juwe, who sat in the remote corners of the venue, could hardly hear the name above the general din; but they joined in the applause anyway. An immaculately dressed, rotund, balding man snuffed out his cigarette, and rolled out from the shadows behind the high table. The MC waved a white handkerchief to the appreciative crowd, and then took over the microphone. Very few could hear his voice over the continuing applause, but all could see him clearly. To Keli, the MC looked surprisingly familiar. Keli stood up briefly from his seat to get a better look. He was involuntarily muttering incomplete sentences, "Is that not...? Could it be...? It must be... Yes it is...Yes it is..."

Yes. It was Mr. Skoop, now introduced by his real surname that had long been corrupted to give him his alias. While the applause continued, Juwe leaned over to Keli and said: "Now we can see whom they chose to be MC. I know him. He's a good man. A good friend of Gordon's."

That was the limit. Keli had had enough. The scales had fallen from his eyes, and he could now see clearly how things worked around here. Dumbfounded and choking with anger, he immediately began to contrive how to extricate himself from this party, which appeared to be a gathering of an ungodly clique. His main objective for coming was obviously unattainable. So, with scant regard for courtesy, Keli informed Juwe that he had to leave immediately. He thrust forth the perfunctory lie that he was expecting an important visitor at his house within the hour. Juwe, out of politeness, did not try to restrain him. He offered to drive Keli back home, and then return to the party. But

Keli would have none of that. In his mind, his break with this group had to be total and final; a clean break. He indicated that he preferred to walk down to the main road where he could easily find a taxi to take him home.

Keli turned his back on Gordon's party. He paced to the main road where he flagged down a taxi.

"Can you take me to Bangumba Street?" Keli asked, as the taxi came to a stop.

"Sure, maza. Get in."

"Thank you."

Once inside the taxi, the driver tried to make small talk, above the din of his blaring radio.

"Evening go good, maza?" the driver commenced in broken English.

"Fine."

"I hear say big, big, party come happen over there. Me hear plenty noise from behind gate."

"Yeah."

"You coming from the party, maza?"

"Somehow."

"How was it, maza?"

"Okay, I guess."

"Me hear owner of that house is big, big man. Plenty money."

"Maybe."

"I sure say food and drink plenty for his party. Me like that kind party. You like, maza?"

"A bit."

The driver at this stage had noticed Keli's reluctance to talk. So, the conversation ceased for a few minutes. Then suddenly, Keli felt an overwhelming desire to walk in the evening air. He felt that he needed the physical exertion to clear his congested mind. He leaned forward from the back seat, tapped the driver lightly on the shoulder, and said, "Can you take me to Wewak Street instead?"

"You talk Bangumba Street, maza."

"Yes, I did. But I changed my mind. It's all in the same direction."

"Okay, maza. Next junction, me turn left."

The taxi discharged Keli at the shopping centre on Wewak Street. Many of the shopkeepers were pulling down their metal blinds for the night. However, he noticed that a small shop across the street was still open for business.

"I wonder if Charlie still sells second-hand books," he said to himself, crossing the street and entering the shop. He greeted Charlie, and proceeded to thumb through a couple of books on sale. None seemed particularly interesting to him, at least not at this time. He popped out of Charlie's shop after a few minutes, and began the half-kilometre walk to Bangumba Street. The therapeutic coolness of the evening air did not disappoint, and by the time he got home, his charged emotions had lost some of their edge.

Dada and the kids had just finished their dinner and were washing up when Keli arrived home.

"That was a very short party," Dada said as she met Keli at the door. "We did not expect you home so soon."

"DD my dear, I had to leave early."

"How come?"

"I'll tell you later. Right now, I'm tired, so tired. I just want to go to bed."

Dada could read from Keli's tone that his mood was abnormal.

"At least, they must have entertained you well," Dada pressed on, eager to figure out what was upsetting Keli.

"I didn't eat anything."

"So, you must still be hungry then, since you didn't eat before going."

"I am not even so sure I have the appetite for anything now."

"Anyway, I'll try and fix something for you while you change."

The conversation was suspended while Keli went upstairs to shed his party regalia. He felt as though he was literally moulting and discarding the paraphernalia in which he had associated with Mr. Skoop and his group. This ritual was part of his resolve to turn his back on them. Meanwhile, Dada cobbled together the semblance of a dinner for Keli.

Half an hour later, while Keli struggled to make himself eat, Dada sat opposite him at the table. She re-opened their suspended conversation.

"So the party was not at all exciting, KK."

"Hmmm." Keli shook his head.

"You had to leave early, you said?" asked Dada, still probing for a meaningful response.

"I had to leave early to save myself from exploding on the spot."

"It was that bad?"

"Yes, it was. Terrible. Terrible."

"What?"

"Terrible."

"Tell me."

"Do you remember who was throwing this party?" Keli asked.

"You said it was the bank official. The one that Juwe introduced us to for the house loan."

"Yes, it was his party. And do you know who the MC was at the party?"

"Juwe. I think they are related."

"Not Juwe. You would never believe who it was."

"Who?"

"The MC was that fraudulent buffoon who is trying to cheat us out of our house."

"You mean that fat fellow who came here with his lawyer?"

"That's the one."

"You mean he knows the bank manager, too?"

"He not only knows him. I hear they are very tight friends. Otherwise, he would not have been chosen to be MC at the banker's party."

"And maybe they are in business together."

"Yes. It is obvious. This banker must be the one who expedited Mr. Skoop's fraudulent scheme to take our house from us for nothing."

"So, just like he operates with Juwe when they give people loans, he operates with Mr. Skoop to prey upon loan defaulters."

"They've got you coming and going. The fellow calls himself a bank manager, but he is a double-dipping daredevil. An idiot. Feeding fat at both ends. You should have seen the palace where he lives on his supposedly meagre salary. And you know what? These crooks all hang together in a clique. A diabolical cartel. The party was full of their types, all in expensive clothing and jewellery. All singing praises from here to eternity, so long as the goodies keep coming. They don't care how the money is earned. All they care is to have plenty of it available for them to enjoy. Oh, all that praise singing for a crook just made me sick."

"Is that why you left?"

"Look, DD. I have taken a decision; an irrevocable decision, and I hope you will join me in it. I have decided to turn my back on that group. Seeing Mr. Skoop on that stage was the straw that broke the camel's back. In fact, I regret having danced along and played their game for so long. Now, they have become my sworn enemies."

"How are you going to fight them? Do you still think we should sue?"

"We don't have the means to sue, as you say. What they have taken from us is lost. But the first step in fighting them is to refuse to continue to play their game. That way, they can no longer fatten themselves from us in future."

"But there will still be enough people ready to play their game. Like all those colleagues in your office who own houses all over the place."

"Yes. Those boys play the game at both ends. They find corrupt ways of supplementing their salaries and making a lot of undeserved money. They can then afford to pay huge mortgages and dole out huge sums in bribes to the likes of Gordon and Mr. Skoop. They take bribes so that they can afford to pay bribes. The two are linked. It's corruption in, corruption out. Easy come, easy go."

"Strange."

"You see; after so many years of resisting, we jumped into the game. But we had one foot in, one foot out. We forgot what the folks say, that if you are going to play with the devil, you had better be a devil yourself. We did what Gordon and Juwe demanded in order to get the loan, but we did not start taking bribes in order to enable us to meet their demands. I did not, and still have not, compromised to the extent of taking bribes to supplement my salary. That is one side of the equation, and I am not ready to give in to that. I know I am in a position of influence, where I could easily compromise myself and get rich. But what would my conscience say?"

"I agree. We should never stoop that low."

"Yes. They may think they are bringing us low by taking our house and driving us to live in the slums, but we will never stoop as low as they stoop to maintain their high life. We are finished with that group for ever. We will now return to where we were prior to our attempt to buy a house."

Dada was overcome with emotion and almost in tears when Keli finished outlining his bravado. They comforted each other in silence for a few minutes. Then they moved over to the bedroom upstairs to continue their emotion-laden discussion. They lay beside each other on the empty bed.

"Do you know something, KK?" asked Dada.

"What?"

"I have also made a resolution similar to yours?"

"What?"

"About a week ago, I started to have second thoughts about my visit to Pastor Emmanuel."

"Oh. The great pastor; your personal miracle worker."

"He certainly didn't work any miracle for us."

"Why do you think his efforts failed?"

"I don't know."

"But you remember what you told me that Maria said."

"Yes, she said that the miracle worked for them."

"No, not that. You remember she said that you have to believe in it for it to work for you? I know you never really believed in all that stuff. You were just doing it out of desperation."

"I think you are right. I had my doubts right from the start. I shouldn't have gone there in the first place."

"What a waste of time."

"When I reflected on the whole thing, it started to look shady to me. Maybe the pastor is just another one of those crooks, trying to make money out of people's misfortunes."

"Who knows? Maybe he actually does miracles for some people, or at least claims to. It surely did not work for us."

"I started to regret that hardship had caused me to abandon our own faith. Adversity forced me to start dabbling in strange things."

"Oh yes. Very strange things. I certainly found them strange, but you seemed so convinced. Where is your talisman?"

"What talisman?"

"The one the pastor gave you to carry around."

"It's not a talisman."

"What is it?"

"It's a holy amulet, that's what he called it. Holy amulet. Anyway, I threw it away last Sunday, shortly after I returned from mass."

"Really! I have to congratulate you for your courage."

"Thank you."

"Yes, we all get tempted from time to time by difficult situations. I'm sure God will forgive you. I myself have already forgiven you. In fact, I never even held it against you."

"Thank you. You're always so understanding."

There was a pause of about a minute, during which each person stared blankly into space.

"So, you are going to let Mr. Skoop and his gang go and enjoy their loot," continued Dada.

"What can I do, DD? We don't have the means to fight them."

After a long pause, Keli added ruefully, "I think we'll move out in a couple of weeks."

Dada burst into tears at the finality of Keli's capitulation. "I and the children have come to love this house," she sobbed. "We have many memories here. Where else can we live as happily?"

"It's not the end of the world, dear," Keli pleaded, pulling her close and wiping her tears. "They may have taken our house, but I can assure that they have not taken over our lives or our spirits."

Again, there was a long silence during which the couple sat clutching unto each other for moral support. When Dada had sufficiently recovered her composure, she asked, "How much do you think that crook paid for this house?"

"I don't know for sure. They refused to tell me. But I've been able to find out."

"How much?"

"I think he paid only ƵƵ20, 000 for the house."

"ƵƵ20,000! He practically got it for free."

"Sure. We all know this house is worth over ƵƵ250,000 now. That's the way they do their thing. It's been a good deal for them. Now, he and his gang will share the profit from the transaction. He gets some; the bank officials get some; the auctioneer gets some; and who knows who else gets some? They are rich, and will keep getting richer at the expense of the poor. There is no middle class anymore. You are either with them, in which case you wallow in wealth; or you are with the struggling impoverished masses."

"Anyway, we've got enough worries. If indeed the house is lost, let's not bother ourselves with how much Skoop paid for it. It's none of our business now."

"Unfortunately, it's still very much our business."

"How?"

"You know our debt at the bank has ballooned considerably. What they are going to do now is to reduce our debt by the amount that Mr. Skoop paid. That will still leave us with nearly ƵƵ200,000 in debt."

"Chei! How on earth are we going to pay that? We will remain debtors all our lives."

"Yes, we've been caught in the debt trap, and there is no escape. That's the way they like it."

"Oh, my God!"

"This really embitters me. It is not just that we lose our house; we are now saddled with a huge debt that we have no reasonable means of paying. Even if we had the means to service the continuing debt, how can I continue to pay debts arising from a house that I no longer own or hope to own? Paying for a house that I live in or hope to own, is one thing; but paying for a non-existent house, with no hope of ultimate ownership, is quite another."

"This is the height of injustice."

"Looking back on the whole business, we would have been better off if we had never ventured to be homeowners. The system in this country is merciless. It wants to consign us to perpetual tenancy. Now it is punishing us for our audacity to think or act otherwise. There is no logic in the whole thing; but that's the way it is."

"There is no justice in this world."

"None at all. Otherwise, how do you explain this situation? After digesting their loot, the bank and its corrupt officials might come after us to recover the rest of our indebtedness. It's tough. Losing the house is not the end of our troubles. It may just be the beginning. Everything we own is now at risk from the creditors. It is not only our house that has been auctioned off. Our entire being is figuratively slated for auction at the unforgiving altar of corruption."

"What a shame."

"As you know, many people in this country have already succumbed in the face of the hard times. They have already auctioned off their souls and consciences to corruption. Even the humble people in all the villages around the nation. They are simply pillaging villagers, if you ask me. All of them have indirectly auctioned off their consciences in connivance with corrupt relatives."

"Like all those villagers who were cavorting and carrying on at Galena's party."

"Yes. They are all part of the problem. If only they would reel in their appetites, and be more questioning of the source of the wealth that their relatives dispense."

"They are all economic scavengers."

"Like Mr. Skoop and his cohorts. All scavengers. They have already made a killing with us. Now they are waiting in the wings to pick through what is left of our decaying economic body."

"God forbid," said Dada instinctively

There was a pause. Then Dada continued.

"Isn't there anything that you people can do about all these dishonest activities?"

"Which people?"

"You people in government."

"I am not in government. I only work for them. I am only a civil servant. The real government is made up of the politicians."

"Politicians."

"Politicians. And you know how they are. Some of them are part of the problem. Some are even worse than the scavengers."

"So, you mean there is no solution, then."

"I think the solution lies at the individual level. Each person has to contribute to the solution in his or her own individual way. The only reason you and I are not in the camp of the scavengers is that your parents and my parents brought us up well. I remember what my father said to me when I went home the other day. He kept saying 'However hungry a man may be, he does not chew his tongue and swallow it. Despite all the troubles, never forget your upbringing.' So, I have always had something to guide me. My duty now is to ensure that Bedemu and all the children are brought up in the same way. That is the way to take care of the future. Even if they can't inherit a house from us, they will inherit high ethical standards. As long as we keep our hands clean, God will continue to bless us and bless them."

"I am sure. Even Bedemu knows that by now."

"Poor Bedemu. I know my running around during this entire crisis has deprived him of my time and attention. I could not even watch Saturday football on television with him today. Did he watch it?"

"Yes. He watched it during dinner time. He had one eye on it and one eye on his food."

"How was the game?"

"I didn't watch, but he said that they showed old games. The national team plays tomorrow, and they will be showing it live. I know you will like to watch."

"Yes," replied Keli.

"Did they win the game they played last week?"

"Yes."

"And do you think they will win again tomorrow?"

"Yes."

There was momentary silence.

"Wait a minute," Dada said. "Did we remember to lock the back door before we came upstairs?"

There was no answer from Keli.

"The back door. Did we lock it?" Dada repeated.

Still no answer. The beleaguered Keli had drifted off into sleep.

Dada groped in the dim bedroom light for a sheet to cover Keli. She then tiptoed downstairs to check the back door. True to her suspicion, they had not locked it. She locked it; then crossed over quietly for a peep into the room where the children slept. All were sound asleep. Dada returned upstairs.

"Keli, sleeping so soundly and snoring?" she muttered to herself. "No more sleepless nights. Thank God."

Dada tucked herself in beside Keli. She soon joined the rest of the family in the land where all afflictions are temporarily forgotten. Sleep had drawn its somnolent healing veil over the entire Alili family and their troubles. All of Zunguzonga sleeps, into a long uncertain night...

Author's postlogue: Did I hear that you are from Zunguzonga?

Humans apart, our main character has been Zunguzonga, the country. It is a country that, paradoxically, is stuck in transit as it attempts the perilous journey from traditionalism to modernity. Nobody knows how long it will remain stagnated in this position, straddling both worlds but unable to reap the full benefits of either. It is like a worker in a large metropolis, who leaves home in the morning driving to work, but gets stuck in an interminable traffic jam. He is unable to get to his destination, yet he is so hemmed in that he is unable to turn around and return home. He is stuck in mid-course, festering and sweltering in the unproductive limbo.

So, you think you know where Zunguzonga is. Our story has told of endemic corruption, chronic poverty, and several other adverse manifestations in Zunguzonga. Your guess is that the country is probably in Africa. Right. But Zunguzonga also exists in South America, in Asia, in the Caribbean, and in the Pacific. For, wherever there are struggling, less developed nations in this world, there too will you find Zunguzonga. Those of us from these regions are indeed from Zunguzonga.

But what about those of us from the developed nations of the world, especially countries in Europe, North America and parts of Asia? We have only seen Zunguzonga on television and in the press. We send aid to it, our multinationals do business there, and we insist on access to its natural resources. But we certainly are not from Zunguzonga. Or are we? Let's see.

When the "innocent" villagers of Zunguzonga enjoy the corrupt earnings of their relatives, and encourage the relatives to bring in more, we marvel at their complicity in corruption. However, when our multinationals exploit and despoil the Zunguzongas of the world, we feign innocence so long as the companies deliver the profits and dividends to us. A similar point could be made for some of the policies of our governments, policies that might favour us in the developed countries, while perpetuating the destitution of Zunguzonga. Are we just as innocently complicitous as the villagers in Zunguzonga? If anything, we are probably more culpable than the villagers are. You see, the villagers in Zunguzonga can claim to be powerless in the face of dictatorships and bad governance. But we, in our democratic system, cannot lay the same claim. We assert that our democracy empowers us to exercise influence over our governments and institutions. Our superior system of governance implies that we – the "innocent civilians" in the developed countries – are each more directly responsible for the benevolence or transgressions of our governments and corporations. To the extent that we sit back and enjoy the fruits of unethical activity, we are no better than the villagers in Zunguzonga. In that sense, we, too, are from Zunguzonga. We too are witnesses to the auction. Have we, or have we not, also been active participants in the auction?

Public Auction

To you that bear the scars of war,
Wounded by greed and graft and more;
To you that strive for conscience clear
Who dare to speak without much fear:
Safeguard, I say, your souls from vile seduction
While most sell theirs in shameful public auction.

I.C. Onwueme (2002)

About the Author

The author has spent a lifetime immersed in the development process in third world countries. Through this, he has acquired a wealth of first-hand experience relevant to the field. With a doctorate degree in agriculture, he has lived and worked as a university professor in Africa, America, Asia/Pacific, and Europe. Having written numerous professional textbooks, he has visited nearly a third of the countries on earth, some of them as a consultant for the United Nations. This global exposure has enabled him to appreciate some of the constraints encountered by developing countries all over the world. In this book, he uses the medium of a novel to analyse these constraints and share his experiences.

Printed in the United States
30537LVS00001B/28